Sally Ann Vollmers

Logistics For You

English for Jobs in Freight-forwarding, Warehousing and Logistics

1. Auflage

Bestellnummer 45007

■ Bildungsverlag EINS

Haben Sie Anregungen oder Kritikpunkte zu diesem Produkt?
Dann senden Sie eine E-Mail an 45007_001@bv-1.de.
Autoren und Verlag freuen sich auf Ihre Rückmeldung.

Die in diesem Produkt gemachten Angaben zu Unternehmen (Namen, Internet- und E-Mail-Adressen, Handelsregistereintragungen, Kontonummern, Steuer-, Telefon- und Faxnummern und alle weiteren Angaben) sind i. d. R. fiktiv, d. h., sie stehen in keinem Zusammenhang mit einem real existierenden Unternehmen in der dargestellten oder einer ähnlichen Form. Dies gilt auch für alle Kunden, Lieferanten und sonstigen Geschäftspartner der Unternehmen wie z. B. Kreditinstitute, Versicherungsunternehmen und andere Dienstleistungsunternehmen. Ausschließlich zum Zwecke der Authentizität werden die Namen real existierender Unternehmen und z. B. im Fall von Kreditinstituten auch deren Bankleitzahlen, IBAN und BIC verwendet.

Die in diesem Werk aufgeführten Internetadressen sind auf dem Stand zum Zeitpunkt der Drucklegung. Die ständige Aktualität der Adressen kann von Seiten des Verlages nicht gewährleistet werden. Darüber hinaus übernimmt der Verlag keine Verantwortung für die Inhalte dieser Seiten.

www.bildungsverlag1.de

Bildungsverlag EINS GmbH
Hansestraße 115, 51149 Köln

ISBN 978-3-427-**45007**-8

© Copyright 2014: Bildungsverlag EINS GmbH, Köln
Das Werk und seine Teile sind urheberrechtlich geschützt. Jede Nutzung in anderen als den gesetzlich zugelassenen Fällen bedarf der vorherigen schriftlichen Einwilligung des Verlages.
Hinweis zu § 52a UrhG: Weder das Werk noch seine Teile dürfen ohne eine solche Einwilligung eingescannt und in ein Netzwerk eingestellt werden. Dies gilt auch für Intranets von Schulen und sonstigen Bildungseinrichtungen.

Vorwort

„Logistics For You" ist die Neubearbeitung unseres erfolgreichen Lehrbuchs „Logistics", das in zehn „Units" alle Aspekte der Spedition, Lagerei und Logistik behandelt, von „A(bfertigung)" bis „Z(usendung)".

Logistik ist ein dynamischer Industriezweig. „Logistics For You", komplett aktualisiert und überarbeitet, reflektiert die vielen wichtigen Entwicklungen der letzten Jahre in dieser Branche.

Dieses Lehrbuch ist für Auszubildende in den Berufen Speditionskaufmann/-frau sowie für Auszubildende der Lagerlogistik gedacht. Praxisnah präsentiert es Dialoge und authentische Dokumente sowie Korrespondenz in realistischen Situationen des Arbeitsalltags des Spediteurs, ob am Hafen, am Flughafen, im Büro eines Logistikunternehmens oder im Lager. Aus Gründen der besseren Lesbarkeit wird bei geschlechtsspezifischen Bezeichnungen in der Regel ausschließlich die männliche Form gewählt.

Der Schwierigkeitsgrad des Buchs entspricht dem des Realschulabschlusses oder des (Abitur- Grundkurses. Die Grammatikbereiche des Buchs wurden so gestaltet, dass sowohl die Grundlagen der englischen Grammatik behandelt werden als auch die Bedürfnisse solcher Schüler befriedigt werden, die bereits über sehr gute Englischkenntnisse verfügen („Fortgeschrittenen-Lesetexte" am Ende des Buchs).

Wie auch in allen anderen Titeln der „For You"-Reihe des Bildungsverlags EINS wurden die Lerneinheiten gemäß den verschiedenen Arten des Fremdsprachenlernens gegliedert: „Comprehension", „Grammar", „Listening", „Activity" und in diesem Fall auch „Vocabulary trainer".

Die „Comprehension"-Einheiten enthalten eine umfangreiche Auswahl verschiedener Texte, von Formularen bis zu geschäftlichen Gesprächen und Zeitungsartikeln, auch die Übungen variieren. Die Grammatikübungen vertiefen die Kenntnisse der grundlegenden Grammatikregeln. Die „Activity"-Einheiten bieten eine Auswahl von Übungen für den aktiven Einsatz der gelernten Sprachelemente: in Arbeits-/Zweiergruppen, in schriftlichen Hausarbeiten oder in Internet-Recherchen. Die „Vocabulary trainer "-Einheiten helfen beim Erlernen der vielen neuen Wörter und technischen Begriffe, welche für den Beruf benötigt werden. Die Vokabellisten am Ende des Buchs sind sowohl nach Lerneinheiten als auch alphabetisch geordnet, mit dem Ziel, den Fachwortschatz der Lernenden zu erweitern.

Wie gewohnt von „Logistics", erklären „Business Tips" einige der alltäglichen Probleme der internationalen Geschäftskommunikation und helfen somit, „Fettnäpfchen" zu umgehen.

Die „Reference Section" vermittelt nützliche Informationen für Logistiker, zum Beispiel Umrechnungstabellen für Zahlen und Maße sowie Ratschläge für die Geschäftskorrespondenz.

Contents

UNIT 1 — Working in the logistics industry .... P. 7

Comprehension	But what is logistics?	P. 7
Comprehension	A job in distribution	P. 8
Activity	My typical day / Identifying vehicles	P. 10
Listening	Job vacancies *(Track 1)*	P. 11
Comprehension	The man who invented containers	P. 11
Activity	Finding answers on the internet	P. 12
Listening	A short history of the Port of Felixstowe *(Track 2)*	P. 13
Activity	Container ports	P. 13
Grammar	Present and past tenses	P. 14
Vocabulary Trainer		P. 15

UNIT 2 — International trade .... P. 17

Comprehension	Why do we need imports and exports?	P. 17
Activity	Where do things come from?	P. 18
Comprehension	Why do we need customs?	P. 19
Grammar	*Some* or *any*?	P. 20
Activity	Personal data	P. 21
Listening	How good is your telephone English? *(Track 3)*	P. 22
Activity	Telephone practice *(role A)*	P. 23
Listening	Telephone dialogues *(Track 4)*	P. 24
Listening	A request for information *(Track 5)*	P. 25
Comprehension	A request for information	P. 25
Listening	A complaint about late delivery *(Track 6)*	P. 26
Comprehension	A complaint about late delivery	P. 26
Activity	Discussing possibilities	P. 28
Comprehension	An important e-mail	P. 29
Activity	Incoterms	P. 30
Comprehension	The answer to the e-mail	P. 31
Grammar	Talking about the future	P. 32
Activity	Telephone practice *(role B)*	P. 33
Vocabulary Trainer		P. 34

UNIT 3 — Surface transport – road and rail .... P. 35

Comprehension	International transport modes	P. 35
Grammar	Comparative and superlative	P. 36
Activity	Presenting a company	P. 37
Comprehension	By road and by rail	P. 38
Activity	Rail freight	P. 40
Grammar	*Must, need* or *have to*?	P. 40
Listening	A quote for a transport job *(Track 7)*	P. 40
Vocabulary Trainer		P. 41
Grammar	The Past Tense and the Present Perfect	P. 41
Comprehension	Thirty years in the road-transport business	P. 42
Vocabulary Trainer		P. 43
Activity	Frequently used sentences in e-mails	P. 44
Comprehension	Regulations for HGVs in the EU	P. 45
Activity	Using the inland waterways	P. 47

UNIT 4 — Sea freight .... P. 48

Comprehension	Sea freight rates	P. 48
Activity	Types of merchant ships	P. 49
Activity	Calculating times of arrival	P. 50

Listening	Specifications on the phone *(Track 8)*	P. 51
Comprehension	Shipping routes	P. 52
Activity	Where is that?	P. 53
Grammar	If-sentences	P. 53
Vocabulary Trainer		P. 54
Comprehension	Shipping marks	P. 55
Activity	Documents required for import	P. 56
Comprehension	IT at the Port of Felixstowe	P. 57
Vocabulary Trainer		P. 58
Activity	Shipping dangerous goods by sea	P. 59

UNIT 5 — Containerisation .... P. 60

Comprehension	An enquiry about container transport	P. 60
Activity	The advantages of containers	P. 61
Listening	Container statistics *(Track 9)*	P. 62
Grammar	The Passive (present tense)	P. 62
Comprehension	Types of containers	P. 63
Activity	Giving precise specifications	P. 64
Vocabulary Trainer		P. 65
Comprehension	Container loads of rubber ducks	P. 65
Activity	Find out for yourself!	P. 66
Grammar	The passive (all tenses)	P. 67
Activity	E-mail correspondence: goods delivery	P. 67
Listening	A delayed consignment *(Track 10)*	P. 69

UNIT 6 — Air freight .... P. 70

Comprehension	AWBs and e-AWBs	P. 70
Activity	Talking about air freight	P. 71
Comprehension	The biggest "fishing port" in Germany	P. 72
Grammar	Commands and requests	P. 73
Activity	How to load a ULD	P. 74
Listening	Work-experience with an IATA agent *(Track 11)*	P. 76
Vocabulary Trainer		P. 77
Activity	International airports	P. 78
Grammar	Prepositions	P. 78
Listening	An air freight quote *(Track 12)*	P. 79
Comprehension	Cargo planes	P. 79

UNIT 7 — Paperwork .... P. 81

Comprehension	FIATA documents	P. 81
Activity	Filling in a personal Customs Declaration	P. 83
Listening	Do we need paperwork? *(Track 13)*	P. 84
Comprehension	A bill of lading	P. 85
Vocabulary Trainer		P. 86
Activity	Filing in a bill of lading / A clean B/L	P. 86
Vocabulary Trainer		P. 87
Comprehension	Claiming on transit insurance	P. 88
Grammar	Politically correct language	P. 89
Vocabulary Trainer		P. 90
Comprehension	Export documents	P. 92
Grammar	Relative clauses: who, which, where or that?	P. 93

UNIT 8 — Warehousing and value-added services .... P. 94

Comprehension	Warehousing then and now	P. 94
Listening	Workstations in the warehouse *(Track 14)*	P. 95
Listening	A liaison meeting *(Track 15)*	P. 95
Activity	Reporting on a meeting	P. 97

Grammar	Present Perfect Continuous	P. 98
Comprehension	The warehouse from hell	P. 99
Comprehension	What does a warehouse worker do?	P. 100
Vocabulary Trainer		P. 101
Activity	A meeting with a customer	P. 102
Grammar	The Past Continuous	P. 103
Activity	Working in warehousing	P. 104

UNIT 9 — Further logistics services and value added services . . . . P. 105

Comprehension	Supply chain management	P. 105
Vocabulary Trainer		P. 107
Listening	Just-in-Time *(Track 16)*	P. 107
Activity	Find out about logistic services	P. 108
Comprehension	Tailor-made logistic solutions	P. 108
Vocabulary Trainer		P. 109
Activity	A real logistic problem	P. 110
Grammar	Adverbs and adjectives	P. 110
Comprehension	Market pressures and "the rag trade"	P. 111
Grammar	Much, many, a lot of	P. 112
Comprehension	Logistics and offshore wind farms	P. 113
Activity	Sources of energy	P. 114

UNIT 10 — A job in an English-speaking country . . . . P. 115

Comprehension	Job advertisements	P. 115
Activity	Jobs in logistics / Career objectives	P. 116
Activity	A Curriculum Vitae	P. 118
Comprehension	The covering letter	P. 119
Activity	Writing a covering letter	P. 120
Listening	Talking about your professional experience *(Track 17)*	P. 121
Activity	Practice for interviews	P. 121
Listening	More interviews *(Track 18)*	P. 121
Grammar	Problems with past tenses	P. 122
Activity	Asking and answering questions	P. 123
Vocabulary Trainer		P. 124
Comprehension	An international management trainee	P. 124

Advanced reading and exercises . . . . P. 126

Comprehension	A report about a distribution problem	P. 126
Activity	Writing reports	P. 128
Activity	Report writing	P. 129
Comprehension	Security in the USA	P. 130
Activity	Security in the USA	P. 132
Vocabulary Trainer		P. 132
Comprehension	Logistics and ecology	P. 133

Reference section . . . . P. 135

Business communications	P. 135
Notes for business letters in English	P. 136
Conversion tables for metric and imperial measures	P. 138
Incoterms 2013	P. 139

Irregular verbs . . . . P. 140

Vocabulary (unit-based) . . . . P. 142

Vocabulary (alphabetical order) . . . . P. 161

Bildquellenverzeichnis . . . . P. 180

UNIT 1:
Working in the logistics industry

But what is logistics?

1 Some people have an old-fashioned view of the freight forwarder's job. They think we must all be either overweight truckers or office workers filling in forms. Well, let me give you an idea of what we really do. In the 21st century, world trade is important for everyone. There was more world trade on just one day in 2010 than for the whole of the year
5 1949 combined. On the one hand, imports mean a bigger selection of goods to buy at lower prices and on the other hand, exports mean more jobs and more money. Can you imagine a supermarket without imported goods, or an automobile manufacturer with no export sales? But who is responsible for getting the goods to the right place at the right time and in good condition? That is the task of logistics, and the job of modern freight
10 forwarders. Logistics controls the supply chain. What does that mean? For the consumer it means for example that the goods he or she wants to buy are available for sale, whether these are fresh food, fashionable clothes, household goods or electronic equipment. For manufacturers, a good logistics service means they do not have to keep big stocks either of raw materials or of finished products, but can still sell many goods to many
15 people.

We modern freight forwarders work together with the manufacturers and sellers to plan the movement of goods with as little loss of time and money as possible, that is, we offer logistic services. We provide warehousing services and organise transport all over the world by sea, air or land, and enter the necessary data into our information systems, so
20 customers can track and trace their consignments, and always know where they are at any time. Maybe we do still sit at our desks, but we do not spend all our time on boring paperwork!

Comprehension

Task 1

Decide whether the statements below are right or wrong, according to the text. If they are wrong, correct them.

a. In the logistics and freight forwarding industry you must be able to drive a truck.
b. Importing and exporting goods means more jobs and opportunities.
c. Many people in the logistics and freight forwarding industry work with computers.
d. World trade has increased by more than 300 % since 1945.
e. Modern international trade could not function without logistics.
f. Logistics companies keep big stocks of goods, so that shops do not need to do this.
g. Freight forwarders offer logistic services and arrange transport.
h. Logistics companies do not need to co-operate with manufacturers and traders.

Task 2

Answer the questions.

a. Why are exports important?
b. Who are the people who profit from efficient supply chain management?
c. What does a forwarder mean when he offers his customers "tracing and tracking"?
d. Which of the tasks mentioned in the text are carried out by the company you work for?

Business Tip!

"Trucker" is an American term which is also often used in popular British English. The correct British English term is "lorry driver" or "long-distance lorry-driver" or "HGV-driver" (HGV stands for "Heavy Goods Vehicle").

A job in distribution

1 My name is Jane Brown. I work for Flingol Ltd., a manufacturing company which produces plastic parts for the automobile industry. I work in the distribution depart-
5 ment. We supply parts to car-manufacturers all over the world on demand. My main task is to deal with exports to customers outside the EU. For example, I am responsible for deliveries to customers in North
10 America. When they send an order, I have to contact freight forwarders or air-freight agents, check schedules, book transport and prepare all the necessary documents.

I like my job, because it is interesting. You have to be able to work with people, and to take decisions. It is important to calculate the costs for transport and to get the job done at the right price and "just-in-time", so that the parts arrive at the assembly line when they are needed. If everything goes well, the automotive company can continue non-stop production, without keeping a big stock of parts. However, if the deliveries do not take place on time the manufacturer will lose a lot of time and money, and our company will lose the contract.

My typical working day is hard to describe, because I do not do the same things every day. There are often problems which I must solve, but my job is never boring. However, I spend many hours sitting at my desk, so I really need to do sport in my free time. I go to the gym at least once a week and in summer I play tennis, whenever I have the time. A lot of my friends play squash, but I don't like it. Most days I get up at 6:30 am and have a good breakfast before I leave the house at about 7:30. I usually go to work by train, and on the way I read the paper or a book. In the evenings when I get home I am usually too tired to go out. David (my boyfriend) often comes home late, and we stay at home and listen to music or watch DVDs, but at the weekend we go to a good restaurant, or visit friends or go to a disco.

I am not working in the office this week, because I am attending a course on new security regulations for shipments to North America. It is quite hard work because there are a lot of rules to learn, but luckily David is not too busy this week, so we can spend more time together. This evening, we are going to a concert.

Comprehension

Task 3

Ask the questions to which the following are the answers.

a. She works for Flingol Ltd.
b. The company produces plastic parts for the automobile industry.
c. She is responsible for deliveries to North America.
d. She likes it because it is interesting.
e. She goes there at least once a week.
f. She gets up at 6:30 in the morning.
g. She goes to work by train.
h. They go to a good restaurant or visit friends.
i. They are going to a concert.

Task 4

Find in the text the English expression for the following:

a. Auf Abruf
b. Hauptaufgabe
c. Teile liefern
d. Verantwortlich für
e. Probleme lösen

Activity

Task 5

Write a description of your own typical day. Your text should give the following information:

When do you get up? Where do you work/go to school? How do you travel to work/school? What do you do every day? Do you like your job/school? Why/Why not? What do you do in your free time? What do you do in the evenings? What are you doing now?

Task 6

Interview your partner: Find out about his/her typical day. Write down ten sentences about his/her typical day compared to your day (e. g. "I get up at 6:30 but she gets up at 7:00"). Tell the class about your partner's day and your day.

Identifying vehicles

Task 7

Below are six pictures of different machines and vehicles used for transporting or handling freight. Match each picture (1–6) to the correct term (a.–f.).

a. forklift truck
b. reach-stacker for containers
c. gantry crane/portal crane
d. delivery van
e. cargo plane
f. heavy goods vehicle

Listening

Job vacancies

Task 8

Listen to track 1.

a. You will hear six job descriptions (1–6). Each job requires experience in driving or operating a vehicle of some kind. Match a job (1–6) with each vehicle above.
b. Listen again. Write down the 6 job titles, 1–6. For example: Job number one is HGV driver/Heavy goods vehicle driver/lorry driver/truck driver

The man who invented containers

1 Malcolm McLean was born on a farm in 1913 and earned his first money selling eggs. When he was fourteen years old, he started work as a gas-station attendant, and soon he saved enough money to buy a second-hand truck. Together with his two brothers he founded the McLean Trucking Company.

5 In 1937 he had the idea of using containers for goods. While he was sitting watching dock workers load the goods from his truck onto a ship, he suddenly thought, "It would be easier to lift my trailer up and put it on board". Based on this idea, his company developed "intermodal boxes" (containers), which could be transported using almost any mode of transport – rail, road or sea. To start with, they used them overland in the USA, where
10 they were very successful.

In 1956, McLean converted a Second World War tanker, Ideal X, into a container-ship for 58 cargo-filled containers. The ship sailed with full cargo from New Jersey to Houston. Later he bought the Pan-Atlantic Shipping Company, changed its name to Sea-Land, and started to haul cargo inside the United States, again with great success.

15 In 1966 his company first carried cargo across the Atlantic in container-ships. They also carried a lot of equipment to South-East Asia during the Vietnam War.

Container transport was cheap, fast and safe, but dock workers didn't like the idea because they were afraid of losing jobs and
20 port officials did not want to invest in the necessary equipment. However it soon became clear the important ports of the future were going to be those which dealt with containers. Now containers are used all over the world.

McLean was a millionaire when he died in 2001 at the age of 87.

Comprehension

Task 9

Ask questions to which the following are the answers. Be careful with tenses.
Example: By selling eggs. How did Malcolm McLean make his first money?

a. On a farm.
b. When he was 14.
c. At a gas-station
d. A second-hand truck
e. The McLean Trucking Company
f. In 1937
g. The name of the containership was Ideal X.

Task 10

Answer the questions.

a. What was the "Ideal X"?
b. How many containers could the Ideal X carry?
c. Where did it sail on its first voyage?
d. Why didn't dock workers like the idea of containers?
e. How old was McLean when he died?

Activity

Finding answers on the internet

Task 11

Use the internet to find out additional facts about McLean.

a. What was the name of the town where McLean was born?
b. What happened on April 26th 1956?
c. What was the name of the first full-celled containership?
d. What was the new name of McLean's company in 1960?

Task 12

Use the internet to find out about the following people: what did they invent, when and where did they live? Choose one of the inventors, and write 100 words about him/her and his/her invention.

Laszlo Biro	Bette Nesbit Graham	Mary Phelps Jacob
Wallace Hume Carothers	James Watt	Ruth Wakefield

The man who invented containers

Business Tip!

Americans write the date differently. They write: month/day/year.
07/01/02 is the first of July 2002. In the European way, the same date would be written: 01.07.02.

Listening

A short history of the Port of Felixstowe

Task 13

Listen to track 2 and answer the questions.

a. Where is Felixstowe and what happens there?
b. Give at least two reasons why Felixstowe is well-positioned to be a transportation hub.
c. How far is Felixstowe from London?
d. Why did the Port of Felixstowe expand in the second half of the twentieth century?
e. How big are the new generation container carriers described in the text?
f. Why can't these ships dock in London?
g. What is a TEU?
h. How much did Hutchinson Whampoa pay for the Port company, and when?

Activity

Container ports

Task 14

a. Visit the Port of Felixstowe website at www.port-of-felixstowe.co.uk.
b. Find out what has happened there since 1994.
c. Find out which other European ports are container ports. Go to the website of one of these ports, and find out more about it. Write a short report on the history, size and use of the port.

Grammar

Present and past tenses

Simple Present	Present Progressive
I/you/we/they come. He/she/it comes. I/you/we/they don't come. He/she/it doesn't come. Do I/you/we/they come? Does he/she/it come?	I am coming, you/we/they are coming. He/she/it is coming. I'm not coming, you/we/they aren't coming. He/she/it isn't coming. Am I coming? Are you/we/they coming? Is he/she/it coming?
Use: for things that always, normally or usually happen.	**Use:** for an event that is happening at this time.
Key words: always, often, sometimes, never, usually, every day, every week	**Key words:** now, at present, today, at the moment, Look! Listen!

Simple Past	
I/you/we/they/he/she/it arrived. I/you/we/they didn't come. He/she/it didn't arrive. Did I/you/we/they arrive? Did he/she/it arrive? (For irregular verbs see the list on page 140)	
Use: for (finished) events which took place in the past.	
Key words: yesterday, ago, last month, last year, in 1860, in the past	

Task 15

Put the verb in brackets into the correct tense: Simple Present, Present Progressive or Simple Past.

John and Eddie both (live) … in London and (work) … for a freight forwarding company. John (work) … in the finance department. He (write) … quotes and (talk) … to customers. Eddie (book) … transport for goods. First he (find out) … about the goods and then he (advise) … the customer on which mode of transport to use. At present he (not/work) … because he is on holiday abroad. He (stay) … in a hotel on Majorca for two weeks. He (sit) … outside a café now, (drink) … coffee and (write) … a postcard to John. John is in his office, he (calculate) … a quote now. He never (take) … his holiday in the summer, because he (love) … skiing, so he always (go) … to the mountains in the winter.

Task 16

Translate into English

a. Er ist gestern angekommen.
b. Wir haben es letzte Woche bestellt.
c. Er arbeitete 2010 in London.
d. Sie sind vor einer Stunde gegangen.
e. Haben Sie uns gestern angerufen?
f. Fuhr er oft nach Berlin?
g. Wir haben das Paket gestern nicht bekommen.
h. Charlie Chaplin wohnte in der Schweiz.
i. Wo ging er zur Schule?
j. Wann hast du ihn zum ersten Mal gesehen?

Task 17

**Ask questions to which the following are the answers. Be careful with tenses.
Example: He came from Berlin. Where did he come from? (From where did he come?)**

a. She worked in Paris.
b. We prepared the documents.
c. The driver drove to the warehouse.
d. She lives in London.
e. Eddie and John play squash on Mondays.
f. My boss checks the quotations.
g. He phoned the customer.
h. The customer is waiting in the office.
i. The secretary was late last week.
j. The goods arrived yesterday morning.

Vocabulary trainer

Task 18

Which word is different? Explain why.

a.	road	rail	air	train
b.	big	small	huge	enormous
c.	modern	new	up-to-date	old-fashioned
d.	dollar	yen	currency	euro
e.	lorry	truck	vehicle	ship
f.	at home	overseas	in foreign countries	abroad

Task 19

Give the verbs for the following nouns. Example: description – describe

loss · delivery · production · warehousing · offer · order · sales · manufacture · preparation

Task 20

Match each term from A with a definition from B.

A	B
A haulier …	… arranges the transport and warehousing of goods, and offers other services, such as packaging.
A forwarder …	… is a cargo of goods that are contained in multimodal boxes.
A logistic services provider …	… is a person or a company that transport goods by road in the service of other companies.
Container freight …	… is cargo consisting of loose, unpackaged commodities in large quantities, for example grain or liquids.
Bulk freight …	… is a flat-bottomed boat that carries cargo on inland waterways.
A container ship …	… is a person or company that acts as an agent to arrange transport of goods from one place to another.
A barge …	… is a cargo-ship specially built to transport cargo only in intermodal boxes or containers.

Business Tip!

"Logistic" is an adjective, meaning "logistisch". "Logistics" is a noun, meaning "Logistik". If you look on the internet you will find "logistic companies" and "logistics companies". Both spellings are correct.

UNIT 2:
International trade

Why do we need imports and exports?

Not many people think about the long journeys many goods travel before they end up in our homes. Why can't we use things which are produced in our country?

The answer to this question is very easy. Most people like a cup of coffee, or tea or hot chocolate for breakfast. What would you drink if none of these products was available? You would have to drink hot milk or herbal tea. Our usual breakfast drinks are imported from distant continents, coffee from South America or Africa, tea from India, Sri Lanka or China and chocolate from South America. Besides, our food would not taste good without spices from far-away countries, like ginger, cinnamon and pepper!

In other cases, foreign companies have know-how that we do not have, or they can produce things more cheaply. The electronic components in your washing machine or computer almost certainly come from Asia, and were imported by a distributing company, who then sold them to the manufacturer of the machine. So even if your machine was "made in Germany", it contains parts which come from abroad. If your car is Japanese or your computer comes from the USA, if you enjoy eating strawberries in winter or like a banana for your lunch, or if you prefer to wear cotton shirts or a cashmere pullover, then you would find it difficult to do without imports. Many German brands would also have to stop production if we closed our ports to foreign goods, because they use imported raw materials or components. Besides, one of the biggest and most important imports is oil. Without it, everything would come to a stand-still. However, it is not difficult to understand that if we import goods, we also need to export our own products in order to maintain the balance of trade. Germany is famous for cars and machinery, and has a good reputation for manufacturing reliable products and for introducing new technology. Exports bring money into the country, and help to improve the economic situation. The logistics industry makes it possible to import and export goods by providing the transport and other essential services, such as warehousing and customs brokerage.

Comprehension

Task 1

Decide whether the statements below are right or wrong, according to the text. Correct those that are wrong.

a. Everybody in modern Europe uses imported products.
b. We could easily do without imports.
c. All tea comes from India.
d. Imports bring more money into the country.
e. A lot of European-made products contain imported parts.
f. German machines have a good reputation.
g. Germany exports large quantities of oil.
h. Logistics plays an important role in international trade.

Task 2

Answer the following questions.

a. Why would our breakfasts be different, if we could not buy imported products?
b. Why is it that, even if you only buy things that say "made in Germany", you cannot avoid all imported products?
c. What is Germany world-famous for?

Task 3

Find words or phrases in the text which mean the same as:

a. specialist skills and expertise
b. computerised parts
c. produced in your own country
d. stop functioning

Activity

Where do things come from?

Task 4

Use the internet to find out from which country or countries the following products <u>originally</u> came from:

a. rubber
b. cane sugar
c. noodles
d. potatoes
e. coffee
f. chocolate

Report back to the class. Your report should be in complete sentences.

Why do we need customs?

Customs is a government agency responsible for controlling the exchange of goods with other countries. The import and export of some goods is forbidden for obvious reasons: these include drugs, such as heroin or cocaine; the movement of other goods is restricted and strictly controlled, such as weapons and nuclear material. The Customs authorities work hard to stop these things being smuggled into or out of their country. Customs officers also check that health and security regulations are complied with and in doing so protect people, animals and plants from disease or criminal activity, and they make sure that import duties are paid.

Customs duties have to be paid on imported goods. We do not have to pay duty on goods that come from another European Union member country, because the EU is a Customs Union – but we do have to pay it on goods from any other country when they enter the EU: for example on imports from the USA, Israel or China. If you bring goods of more than a certain value home from a holiday in the USA, you will have to declare them when you go through Customs. If your company imports goods from outside the EU, they have to be cleared through Customs, too. Until they have been cleared, dutiable goods can be held in a bonded store at the port or airport of arrival.

Customs duties create revenue for the State and protect domestic industry and agriculture. Another way to protect producers in the country is to introduce a quota system. This was used, for example, to limit the number of Japanese cars imported to the UK and to the US at the end of the twentieth century. A quota is set, that means a quantity is agreed for any one product, and only this set quantity can enter the country.

Internationally, the Customs tariffs are based on the World Customs Organisation's classification of goods, which is called the Harmonised Commodity Description and Coding System. This system is used for example by the EU, Australia, Canada, Singapore and the USA. Different kinds of goods have different duty tariffs, but the duty is usually a percentage of the value of the imported articles.

Comprehension

Task 5

Answer the questions.

a. Name a commodity that cannot normally be imported or exported.
b. Name two other types of goods on which there are import/export restrictions.
c. What other things do the Customs Authorities do besides stopping smugglers?
d. Why don't you have to pay duty on goods imported into Germany from the UK?
e. What is the name of the tariff system used by Customs in the USA and the EU?
f. Where are imported goods kept until they have been cleared through Customs?
g. Explain what is meant by a "quota system".
h. Do all countries in the world use the same coding system for classifying goods?

Task 6

Find words in the text that mean the same as:

a. guns
b. illnesses
c. income

Grammar

Some or any?

| **Some:** in a positive sentence
He ordered some goods. | **Any:** in a negative sentence or a question
We didn't order any goods. Did they order any goods? |

The same rule applies to something/anything, someone/anyone, somebody/anybody, somewhere/anywhere.

Exceptions

| **Some:** is correct when the "question" is really an offer of something, not a request for information.
Would you like some coffee? | **Any:** can be used in a positive sentence in the sense of „jeder beliebiger".
Any time will suit me, come when you can. |

Task 7

State whether the correct form is "some" or "any" for (1) - (10) in the dialogue below.

Customs Officer: Good morning. Have you got …(1)… thing to declare? Did you buy …(2)…thing in the US? Have you brought …(3)… gifts with you?

Traveller: No, I don't have …(4)… gifts. And I only bought some books. But I have …(5)… samples of cloth with me. I am an agent for a company that makes cotton cloth. Here, look.

Customs Officer: That is OK, Sir, you don't have to pay …(6)… duty on them. Would you open your other case, please? What is that? You have …(7)… cigars. 200 expensive cigars.

Traveller: Yes, but I didn't buy them in the US. They are from Cuba.

Customs Officer: May I give you …(8)… advice? Don't try to be funny.

Traveller: I'm not trying to be funny…(9) …body told me I could bring 200 cigars in with me. For personal use.

Customs Officer: …(10)…body with a bit of sense knows you can only bring in 50 cigars. These are confiscated. And there will be a fine to pay.

Activity

Personal data

Task 8

Read the information on the cards as you would say it to an English-speaking person (see page 135 for spelling).

Nordstar Logistik GmbH
Marcus Müller
Verkaufsdirektor
Grünenbergstraße 15
65555 Limburg a. d. Lahn
Fon (+49) (0)6431 135 237
Fax (+49) (0)6431 135 196
E-Mail: marcus.mueller2@nordstar.com

Smith Optics plc
Ann Griffiths
Procurement Manager
216, Ipswich Road
London W11 4UA
Tel (+44) 1191 8834 775
Fax (+44) 1191 8 8834 771
E-Mail ann_griffiths@newjag.co.uk

Task 9

Make up a company name, address and telephone number. Dictate them to your partner. Check for mistakes.

Business Tip!

@ = at
. = dot
/ = slash
– = dash (minus)
_ = underscore
underline

Give phone numbers in single digits, not in pairs: 25 83 = two five eight three.
Do not to use the German spelling alphabet without saying the letters, as Germans often do. If, when making an appointment, a German visitor spells her first name, Lea, "Ludwig Emil Anton", an English person will think that three men are coming.

Listening

How good is your telephone English?

Task 10

Listen to track 3 and check your pronunciation of the phrases. Match an English phrase from column B to each German translation in column A.

A	B
Ich stelle durch.	She is having lunch.
Er ist zur Zeit nicht erreichbar.	He'll call you back.
Sie ist zu Tisch.	You can reach him on his mobile (phone).
Tut mir leid, ich habe mich verwählt.	Please give him a message.
Wie kann ich Ihnen helfen?	Speaking.
Am Apparat.	Please ring again later.
Mit wem wollen sie sprechen?	How can I help you?
Wollen Sie warten?	Do you want to hold on?
Bitte rufen Sie später wieder an.	Do you want to leave a message?
Er ruft zurück.	I'll put you through.
Ich verbinde.	The line is busy.
Er spricht gerade.	Sorry, (I dialled the) wrong number.
Die Leitung ist besetzt.	I'll connect you.
Wollen Sie eine Nachricht hinterlassen?	He is not available now.
Bitte geben Sie ihm eine Nachricht.	The line is engaged.
Sie können ihn auf seinem Handy erreichen.	Who would you like to speak to?

Business Tip!

Remember, when a caller asks for you by name on the phone, do not answer "I'm on the phone"! English-speakers would understand that you were busy on another line and could not speak to them. The correct form is "Speaking".

Activity

Telephone practice *(role A)*

Task 11

Work with a partner. Partner A works from this page. Partner B turns to page 33.

Create dialogues in English, by following the instructions for your two roles. Read your own role through before you begin.

<u>Do not</u> translate the instructions into German: imagine these are real conversations. Think what you would say in English in the situation described.

Dialogue 1

Partner A: Ihr Name ist Simon(e) Smith. Sie arbeiten bei Wilhelmsohn Logistik GmbH.

Das Telefon klingelt.

A   Antworten Sie. Sagen Sie, wer Sie sind. Fragen Sie, was der Anrufer möchte.
B   …
A   Sie versuchen durchzustellen.
B   …
A   Die verlangte Person ist nicht an ihrem Platz.
B   …
A   Sie kennen deren Handynummer nicht.
B   …
A   Frau Green sollte bald im Büro sein. Sie fragen, ob der Anrufer eine Nachricht hinterlassen möchte.
B   …
A   Sie notieren den Namen und die Firma: Bei Unsicherheiten sollten Sie den Anrufer bitten, etwas zu wiederholen oder ein Wort zu buchstabieren. Sie fragen nach der Telefonnummer.
B   …
A   Wenn Sie nicht sicher sind, die Nachricht richtig verstanden zu haben, fragen Sie nach. Wenn Sie sich sicher sind, verabschieden Sie sich mit dem Versprechen, die Nachricht weiterzuleiten.

Dialogue 2

Partner A: Ihr Name ist Paul(a) Brown. Sie arbeiten bei Jarmyn GmbH.

A   Rufen Sie Freight Line Ltd an.
B   …
A   Sie wollen mit Chris Black sprechen. Melden Sie sich mit Namen und Firma.
B   …
A   Sie sagen, wie es Ihnen geht, und fragen höflich nach Ihrem Partner.
B   …
A   Sie möchten ein Angebot für den Transport (per Luft) von fünf Kisten (je 85 kg) Elektronikteile von Hongkong Flughafen nach Frankfurt Flughafen. Die Teile werden nächsten Mittwoch (geben Sie das Datum an) in Hongkong geliefert und müssen bis Freitag Mittag in Frankfurt sein.

B ...
A Sie möchten, dass das Angebot per E-Mail geschickt wird. Ihre E-Mail Adresse ist: p.brown@jarmyn.com.
B ...
A Sie bestätigen.
B ...
A Wiederholen Sie die Informationen, die verlangt werden.
B ...
A Sagen Sie, dass die Angaben korrekt sind, oder korrigieren Sie.
B ...
A Verabschieden Sie sich.

Expression Bank

It is urgent	Es ist dringend
I am afraid/I'm sorry	Leider/Es tut mir leid
quote	Preisvorschlag
to confirm	bestätigen
consignment	Sendung
offer	Angebot
case	Kiste
to promise	versprechen

Listening

Telephone dialogues

Task 12

Listen to track 4. Compare your dialogues from Task 11 to the ones you hear.

Listening

A request for information

Task 13

Listen to track 5, then answer the questions below. Do not read the text yet.

a. What is the name of the caller?
b. Who does he want to talk to?
c. Where does the caller want to go and what does he want to do there?
d. Why has he made this call?
e. Can Magda tell him what he wants to know?

Now read the text.

A request for information

1 Magda Braun: Nord-Atlantik Logistik. Braun.
  Paul: Hello. Can I speak to Magda?
  Magda: Oh, hi Paul. Magda speaking. How are you today?
  Paul: Hello, Magda. I'm fine, thanks. How are you doing?
5 Magda: I'm just fine, too, Paul. It's lovely weather here today.
  Paul: You are lucky then. It's pouring down with rain here.
  Magda: Then I hope the rain will soon stop. How can I help you, Paul?
  Paul: Well, I'm phoning because I want to ask you a personal favour, I mean, it has nothing to do with work.
10 Magda: Yes? Please go on.
  Paul: I wonder if you can help me, if it isn't too much trouble. You see, my hobby is motorbikes, Harley Davidsons, and a group of us would like to take our own bikes to the U.S. and ride down Route 66.
  Magda: That sounds fantastic. You'd see the real America!
15 Paul: Yes, it's a dream of mine! What I wanted to ask you is, is it true that your company specialises in transporting bikes across the Atlantic?
  Magda: Yes, that's right. We ship a lot of bikes to the US and back.
  Paul: Well, you see, our customised bikes are very valuable. The transport company must know how to pack them safely, and must not take any risks.
20   Could you possibly tell me about the transport arrangements?
  Magda: You needn't worry. I know the bikes are specially packed so they can't be damaged. But it is a separate department, so I can't tell you the details of the scheme.
  Paul: Would you mind sending me some information?
25 Magda: No, of course not. You could get some information from our website, of course, if you click on "extra services" but I'll give your address to the head of the department and he'll put a brochure in the post for you. Sorry, I'll have to hang up now, there is someone on the other line. Bye.
  Paul: Goodbye Magda, and thanks for your help.

Comprehension

Task 14

Answer the following questions.

a. What is the purpose of the first part of their conversation?
b. Why does Magda end the conversation?
c. Why can Magda not tell Paul what he wants to know?
d. What will she do for Paul?
e. Why does he want a specialised company to transport the bikes?
f. Where else could he get the information he needs?

Listening

A complaint about late delivery

Task 15

Listen to track 6. Do not read the text in your book yet. Listen again, and answer the questions below.

a. Have the boots which were ordered arrived?
b. What does Paul decide to do?
c. What must he do to dial the company?
d. What is the name of the company he is phoning?
e. Why does nobody answer the phone?
f. When he rings again, does he get through to the right person immediately?
g. What is his order number?
h. When was the order dispatched?
i. What is Clive's extension number?

Now read the text.

A complaint about late delivery

The caller is Paul Smith, purchasing manager for Big Foot Fashions, a chain of shoe-shops with branches in all big towns in the UK.
Paul and his assistant Ann are in the office at the headquarters of Big Foot Fashions.

1 Paul: Has that consignment of Bush boots arrived yet?
   Ann: No, unfortunately it hasn't, Paul. The managers of several of our stores are complaining because customers are asking for them. They really are in demand! And if the kids can't buy them in our stores, then of course they go elsewhere!
5 Paul: Well, I don't see why we should lose custom just because our supplier doesn't deliver on time. I'm going to ring them up and say what I think of them! What is the dialling code for the US, Ann?
   Ann: Just press 9. Our suppliers' numbers are programmed into the phone.
   Paul: Oh yes, of course.

A complaint about late delivery

10	Phone:	This is the Bush Boots Company. Our office hours are from 9:00 am to 5:00 pm. Please leave a message. We will call you back.
	Paul:	Bother, there is no-one in the office.
	Ann:	Well, I think it is only about 8:00 in the morning over there. Why don't you try in about an hour?
15	Paul:	In about an hour? Right.
		...
	Paul:	Well, the Bush Boots people should be in by now. Here goes.
		(dials, phone rings)
	Phone:	You are connected to the Bush Boots Company. Please hold the line.
20	Paul:	Bother! This call is costing me a fortune!
	Phone:	Good morning. How may we help you?
	Paul:	I'm ringing from the UK. I'm Paul Smith, from Big Foot Fashions, and I want to ask about our last order.
	Phone:	One moment please, I'll put you through to Export. Please hold the line.
25		Sorry, the line is busy. I'll put you on hold.
	Paul:	No, I don't want to hold on, I ... Oh bother. Now how long will I have to wait?
	Phone:	Hello. Export Department. Mary-Jo here. How may I help you?
	Paul:	Quickly, please. I'm calling from Europe. I'm Paul Smith from Big Foot Fashions in the UK and ...
30	Mary-Jo:	Please tell me your order number.
	Paul:	Oh, erm ..., hang on a minute, oh yes: zero three slash eight five four slash B
	Mary-Jo:	Just one minute there, Paul. I'll transfer the call.
	Phone:	Hello. Clive Dexter here.
	Paul:	Paul Smith speaking from Big Foot Fashions, UK.
35	Clive:	Hello Paul. Nice to speak to you. Are you happy with the selection of fashion boots that we sent you last month?
	Paul:	No, I am not. I mean, we have not received delivery from your company, and our shop managers are complaining they are losing customers. We have advertised your product, and now people are asking where the boots are. In fact, it
40		just isn't good enough.
	Clive:	Well, Paul, I am very sorry to hear that. Could you wait just a moment while I check it on my computer? Yes, there it is, Big Foot Fashions. The consignment was dispatched on March 18th. As your company requested, we sent them via the Port of Felixstowe. Ah yes, they were shipped on the MS Lady Jane, date of
45		arrival, March 23rd.
	Paul:	Well, they never got here.
	Clive:	That is a problem. Look, I'll try to find out what I can from this end. Would you mind contacting your British freight forwarding company and seeing if they can give you any information? I'm sure we can find out what happened,
50		Paul.
	Paul:	I certainly hope so. And without spending a fortune on phone bills.
	Clive:	What? Oh, don't you have my extension number? Just dial 345 at the end of the number instead of double zero, and you dial me direct.
	Paul:	Thanks, I'll do that. Goodbye.

Comprehension

Task 16

After you have read the text, answer the following questions.

a. Why is it important that the consignment of Bush boots should arrive very soon?
b. Why doesn't Paul need to dial the whole number for his American business partners?
c. Why doesn't anyone answer the phone?
d. How many people does Paul speak to before he gets through to Clive?
e. Where were the boots sent to?
f. How can Paul get through to Clive more quickly in future?
g. What does Clive ask Paul to do?

Business Tip!

Especially in the USA, but also in the UK, many people do not use the 24-hour clock.
From 12:00 midnight to 12:00 midday is "am"; 2:00 am is 02:00.
From 12:00 midday to 12:00 midnight is "pm"; 2:00 pm is 14:00.
Remember if you phone the USA, there is a time difference of at least 6 hours. Make sure you phone during office hours.

Activity

Discussing possibilities

Task 17

What could have happened to the consignment? Here are some suggestions.
- The consignment was not sent off from the US.
- The boots were lost or stolen on board the ship.
- They arrived at the Port of Felixstowe, but were sent to the wrong address.
- They are still waiting at the Port, because they have not been cleared through customs.
- …

What do you think? Discuss with your partner.
- I don't think/think the consignment was … because …
- Maybe the boots were …, but it is unlikely, because …
- I don't think they were … because …
- So the boots must be …

An important e-mail

Paul contacted his forwarder, Tim Fuller. Tim told him he had sent him an e-mail some days earlier about the consignment. Paul had not read it because he did not recognise the address and he thought it was "spam". Now he has recovered it from the trash folder. Here is the e-mail.

From: tfroadtrans@logisticsolutions.co.uk
To: psmith@bigfootfash.co.uk
Cc:
Subject: Your consignment NY563

Hi Paul,

Please note my new e-mail address. You will find that all our e-mail addresses in the company have been changed according to a new system.

Your consignment NY 563 of ten pallets of footwear arrived from New York today on the MV Lady Jane. It was dispatched DAT and is being held at the port terminal. I accepted responsibility for the consignment, but it will cost £656.00 to clear it through customs. In addition, I need a copy of your original order, if possible. The Customs officer here wants to check it against the commercial invoice. It's OK, I don't think there is a problem here.

Please get in touch asap, and then I can send the goods on to you by road immediately.

Best regards,
Tim Fuller

Comprehension

Task 18

Read the text "An important e-mail" and answer the following questions.

a. Why didn't Paul open the e-mail?
b. Did the American seller of the boots make any mistake?
c. Why can't the forwarder pick up the boots and deliver them?
d. What does MV stand for?
e. What does DAT stand for? (If you do not know, see below under "Incoterms".)

Business Tip!

Some short forms are commonly used in e-mails, for example "asap" for "as soon as possible". Others, like "CU" for "see you", are more suitable for private communications.

Activity

Incoterms

Task 19

DAT is an Incoterm. It stands for "delivered at terminal".

Look up Incoterms on the internet, on an English-language site. Find out which of the following statements are true, and which are untrue. Correct those that are wrong.

a. There are 11 Incoterms now.
b. There were fewer Incoterms before 2010.
c. Incoterms can be four letters.
d. DDP means that the goods are "delivered duty paid".
e. Incoterms are used in contracts for the sale of goods from one country to another.
f. When were the Incoterms last updated?

An important e-mail   31

The answer to the e-mail

From: psmith@bigfootfash.co.uk
To: tfroadtrans@logisticsolutions.co.uk
Cc:
Subject: Re: Your consignment NY563

Hi Tim,

Sorry it took so long to answer your e-mail. Please get customs clearance and send the consignment on. I need it yesterday!

For a copy of the order, see below.

Best wishes,
Paul Smith

Quantity	Article number	Description	Price	VAT	Total
300 pairs	U/20	Texan Leather Boots (sizes 7-14)	$20.00	0 %	$6,000.00
100 pairs	P/301	Texan Canvas Boots (sizes 8-14)	$15.50	0 %	$1,500.00
500 pairs	IJ-R/120	Boots an' spurs (sizes 7-15)	$50.00	0 %	$25,000.00
		Final Total (incl. 0 % VAT)			$32,500.00

(Prices DAT Felixstowe)

Comprehension

Task 20

Answer the following questions below.

a. What does Paul want Tim to do?
b. How many pairs of boots has Paul bought?
c. Which sort of boots are the most expensive?
d. How much does the whole order cost? (Write the sum out.)
e. Is the Customs Duty for importing the boots into the UK included in this sum?
f. Is there any VAT (Value Added Tax) to pay on the boots?

Grammar

Talking about the future

1) "Will" or "(be) going to"?

Will-Future = I/you/he/she/it/we/you/they + will + verb
I will be on holiday next week.
It will be sunny in Spain.
We'll have a good time.
Will it rain tomorrow? Will they buy more goods next year?
It will not rain tomorrow. Short form: It won't rain.

Use
1. for forecasts: *There will be snow in Scotland.*
2. for saying what you think, hope or fear will happen: *He thinks things will get worse, but I hope they will improve.*
3. for actions which will follow as a result of something in the present: *Can I speak to John? – Yes, I'll connect you. I have a headache. – I'll give you an aspirin. That will make it better.*

Going-to-Future = I am going/he/she/it is going/you/we/they are going to + verb
It is going to rain.
Are you going to come home now?
They aren't going to do it.

Use
1. for saying what you intend to do: *The service is very bad. I'm going to complain about it.*
2. for stating that an event is definitely going to happen: *It looks very stormy! – Yes, it is going to rain.*

In many cases, "going to" or "will" are both possible.
In the case of the verb "go", the present continuous (be+verb+ing) often replaces the going-to-future. *Where are you going on holiday this summer? – I'm going to France.*

2) "Will" or "want to"/ "like"/ "would like"?

will = wird/werden I will go. = Ich werde gehen.	want to = will/wollen I want to go. = Ich will gehen.
like = mag/mögen I like tea. = Ich mag Tee.	would like = gerne möchten I'd like a cup of tea. = Ich möchte gerne eine Tasse Tee.

Task 21

Complete the sentences with will-future or going-to-future.

a. Tomorrow …(1)… be a cold and rainy day.
b. It is so cold that I'm certain it…(2) … snow.
c. I need the file. – OK, I …(3)… get it for you.
d. What (you/do) at the weekend? – I …(4)… go home and see my parents.
e. Look out! That ladder is not safe! It …(5)… to fall down!
f. My friend thinks he …(6)… be able to come.
g. I hope there (not/be)…(7)… any more wars in my lifetime.
i. I always tell myself: "I …(8)… win."

Task 22

Translate into German:

a. I will send the goods next week.
b. He wants to go home now.
c. We like our new car.
d. I'd like a new car.
e. We won't go to the disco.
f. We want to have a party next week.

Activity

Telephone practice *(role B)*

Task 23

Work with a partner. Partner A works from page 23. Partner B works from this page. Create dialogues in English, by following the instructions for your two roles.
Read your own role through before you begin. <u>Do not</u> translate the instructions into German: imagine these are real conversations. Think what you would say in English in the situation described. Check the written messages at the end of each conversation. Did you get them right?
When you have finished the dialogues, listen to them. (There is usually more than one way of asking or answering, so if your version is not exactly the same as the audio, it does not mean it must be wrong. Ask your teacher.)

Dialogue 1

Partner B: Ihr Name ist Ramona Singh und Sie arbeiten bei Handwork from India Ltd.

B	Sie rufen bei Wilhelmsohn Logistik GmbH an. Stellen Sie sich vor. Sie wollen mit Mrs Green sprechen.
A	…
B	Sie bedanken sich.
A	…
B	Sie sagen, es ist dringend, und fragen nach ihrer Handynummer.
A	…
B	Sie sagen, sie brauchen eine schnelle Antwort.
A	…
B	Sie hinterlassen folgende Nachricht: Frau Green solle Sie (Ramona Singh, Handwork from India GmbH), bitte so schnell wie möglich anrufen. Buchstabieren Sie Ihren Nachnamen.
A	…
B	Geben Sie A Ihre Telefonnummer: 02478572234. Erklären Sie, dass es um die letzte Sendung aus Delhi geht.
A	…
B	Wenn A Fragen hat, beantworten Sie sie. Wenn alles klar ist, bedanken und verabschieden Sie sich.

Dialogue 2

Partner B: Ihr Name ist Chris Black. Sie arbeiten bei Freight Line Ltd.

Das Telefon klingelt:

B   Sie sagen „Guten Tag" und nennen den Namen Ihrer Firma.
A   …
B   Sie sagen „Am Apparat", und erkundigen sich nach dem Wohlbefinden Ihres Gesprächpartners.
A   …
B   Sie antworten, dass es Ihnen gut geht, und fragen, was Sie für den/die Anrufer(in) tun können.
A   …
B   Es tut Ihnen leid, aber zurzeit ist ihr PC nicht in Ordnung. Sie könnten das Angebot in etwa einer Stunde per Telefon abgeben.
A   …
B   Sie sind einverstanden, das Angebot so schnell wie möglich per E-Mail zu senden (notieren Sie die E-Mail-Adresse).
A   …
B   Falls Sie die Daten für das Angebot noch nicht aufgeschrieben haben, fragen Sie danach und schreiben sie diese auf.
A   …
B   Verabschieden Sie sich und entschuldigen Sie sich dafür, dass Sie das Angebot nicht sofort machen können. Versprechen Sie, es so bald wie möglich zu erledigen.

When you have finished work on the dialogues, turn back to page 23.

Vocabulary trainer

Task 24

The expressions below are to be found in the texts of this lesson. Can you remember the corresponding English expressions? Please translate.

a. Ich habe eine persönliche Bitte an Sie.

b. Wenn es nicht zu viele Umstände macht.

c. Sie brauchen sich keine Sorgen zu machen.

d. Hinterlassen Sie bitte eine Nachricht.

e. Es kostet ein Vermögen.

f. Ich setze Sie in die Warteschlange.

UNIT 3:
Surface transport – road and rail

International transport modes

An important part of the traditional role of the freight forwarder is to advise exporters on the most suitable modes of transport for their goods. He then arranges transport by booking space with carriers by sea, road, rail or air. Carriers are companies which carry out the actual transport jobs, whether they are air-freight lines, road hauliers, shipping lines or railway companies. Some logistics companies also act as hauliers.

The choice of the mode of transport depends on a number of factors, including, of course, both the nature of the goods (weight, size, value, whether they are perishable or fragile etc.) and their destination.

Air transport is the fastest, but costs a lot more than surface transport. To give you an idea of the transport times, let us look at three ways of transporting goods from Hamburg to San Francisco: by air freight, you could reckon about two days at the most. By multi-modal transport, that is, sea freight to New York and then by rail from New York to San Francisco, it would take altogether approximately 20 days, whereas by sea freight Hamburg – San Francisco (via the Panama Canal), it would take 28 days. Air transport is used, for example, to fly cut flowers from Columbia to Paris or fish from Asia to Frankfurt because they are perishable goods and speed is essential. It would cost too much to fly in cars or automobile parts from Japan. They travel by sea.

Products of all kinds are transported by sea. Mostly they are packed into containers and carried on container ships, although bulk goods, such as grain, coal, metal ores and oil are carried in specially built bulk vessels. Overland in Europe, a much higher proportion of freight travels by road than by rail, with only a small percentage of heavy bulk goods being carried in barges on the inland waterways. In the USA, a much greater number of goods are carried by rail. Both road and rail transport involve a lot of container traffic. Containerisation makes multi-modal transport a possibility. Containers can be transferred from road to ship or from road to rail, etc. If you look at the example above of transport times from Hamburg to San Francisco, you will see one of the main advantages of multi-modal transport.

Comprehension

Task 1

Answer the following questions.

a. What is the difference between a freight forwarder and a carrier?
b. What does a haulier do?
c. Which of the following statements is correct:
   - Perishable goods, like glasses, are easily breakable.
   - Perishable goods, for example fresh food, go bad if kept too long.
   - Perishable goods must be kept frozen.
d. Which is the slowest way to send goods from Germany to San Francisco?
e. What kinds of goods are not carried in containers on container ships? Give two examples.
f. Which mode of transport is the most used in Europe, road or rail?
g. What is different in the USA?
h. Name two possible means of transport for bulk cargo in Europe.
i. What is meant by "multi-modal transport"?
j. State one advantage of multi-modal transport.

Task 2

Find the words or phrases in the text with the following meanings.

a. A company which specialises in carrying goods by air.
b. A company which owns ships that are used to carry freight.
c. The place where goods are to be delivered.
d. Transport by sea and road, or by air and road, or by rail and sea, etc.
e. Transport by land and sea.
f. Goods that can very easily get broken.
g. A set of transport processes which is provided for a specific customer to fit his needs.

Grammar

Comparative and superlative

adjective + -er/-est

All adjectives on one syllable: *cheap – cheaper – cheapest*
Two-syllable adjectives ending in -y: *pretty – prettier – prettiest*

Note the spelling: *pretty – prettier; fat – fatter*

more/most + adjective

all other two-syllable adjectives: *careless – more careless – most careless*
all adjectives with more than two syllables: *expensive – more expensive – most expensive*

Negative comparison: less/least + adjective

For a negative comparison: *big – less big – the least big; hot – less hot – the least hot*

International transport modes

Exceptions

good – better – best
bad – worse – worst

Use

*Transport by air is **faster than** surface transport.*
*The Airbus A380 is **the** big**gest** aircraft in the world.*
*He is not **as** tall **as** his brother.*

Task 3

What are the missing words in the sentences below?

a. The passage through the Channel Tunnel is faster …(1)… the crossing on a ferry.
b. The United States is bigger …(2)… Europe.
c. When I buy an articulated truck, I want …(3)… best one on the market.
d. Is your motorbike as fast …(4)… my car?
f. Microsoft is the …(5)… biggest software company in the world.
g. That is too expensive. I want something cheaper …(6)… that.
h. PCs are easier to use now …(7)… in the 1980s.
i. Their technology is not as up-to-date …(8)… ours.
j. Air transport is …(9)… expensive than surface transport.

Task 4

Give the correct forms of the words in brackets.

a. Surface transport is (slow) than air freight.
b. Silver is (valuable) than copper, but gold is (valuable).
c. Australia is (far) from Europe than Egypt.
d. I think in this case rail transport would be (good) than road.
e. Is diesel oil as (dangerous) as petrol?
f. He is the (nice) man I have ever met.
g. The weather today is (bad) than it was yesterday.
h. Their truck is (big) than our lorry.
i. If you eat all that, you will get (fat) than you are now.
j. That is the (silly) thing I have ever heard.

Activity

Presenting a company

Task 5

Read the short report about an imaginary company. Each sentence is the answer to a question beginning with "Where …", "When …" "What …" and "How …". Write a question for each sentence.

The name of the company is Unibrit Ltd. Its headquarters are in Kent. It was founded in 1990. The aim of the company is to offer integrated transport and logistics services worldwide. Its services include road, rail, sea and air-freight services worldwide, warehousing services and import-export support. Customers can get online quotes for services, and can trace and track their consignments.

Task 6

Visit the website of a logistics company. Click on the English Language version. Write a similar short report about a real company. Answer all the questions that you wrote down in Task 5.

Business Tip!

Words like "company", "family" or "team" which stand for a group of people can be used with a singular or a plural verb, and can be replaced by "it", "they", or, if you belong to the particular company or group, "we".
Examples: "The company offers logistics solutions." – "They offer logistics solutions." – "It is/they are the best in their field."

By road and by rail

1   Anywhere in Western Europe you will see a large number of freight vehicles on the main roads, including delivery vans, pick-up trucks, and, above all, semi-trailers (in
5   the UK these are called articulated lorries). The EU has introduced strict regulations on the maximum weight, dimension and road-worthiness of trucks, on how loads must be secured and on the number of hours drivers
10 are allowed to drive before they must take a break. Police continually check on trucks and drivers, and heavy fines can be imposed on drivers or on their companies if they break the rules.

15 The number of heavy goods vehicles (HGVs) is increasing, although the costs of road freight are also steadily rising. Diesel is no longer an inexpensive fuel and many European countries charge a heavy toll for the

use of their main roads. Germany has introduced a lorry toll for using its motorways. If you add these costs to the maintenance of the vehicles, the drivers' pay and the almost inevitable fines for speeding or for neglecting rest periods (with a tight time-schedule, any traffic hold-up puts drivers under pressure), then the basic costs of road transport are high even before the company begins to make a profit. In many cases, however, there is no alternative to road transport. Rail networks in Europe are not as flexible as road transport so the costs of transhipment of the goods from the railway station to the destination can be high and time can be lost. Besides, there can be problems when passing from one country to another: some Eastern European countries have a different rail track gauge: that means that the distance between the rails is different, and so goods must be transferred to different trains. In the USA things are different. Freight train shipments carried 38 % of US freight in 2000 as compared to only 8 % in Europe. There are historical and economic reasons for this difference. Long-distance passenger trains have lower importance in the US, so freight has priority. Railways across the whole of the US have the same gauge, and are constructed to allow the use of double-stack cars, or wagons that can carry two standard containers one on top of the other, allowing considerable savings on freight costs. Local railway networks allow more flexibility in pick-up and delivery services.

All types of commodities can of course be carried by rail, but a high percentage of rail freight both in Europe and in America consists of dry bulk cargo, that is, goods such as coal, iron ore, cement or loose grain that are shipped unpacked in large quantities. In parts of Europe, America and Russia many such cargos are carried by barges on inland waterways, but canal or river transport is not often used commercially in the UK.

If more European freight was carried by rail, there would be less traffic on Europe's roads, less fuel would be consumed, and there would be less damage to the environment. Higher use of the inland waterways would mean greater reduction in fuel consumption and pollution. However, the majority of freight continues to travel by road.

Comprehension

Task 7

Decide which statements are true according to the text. Correct the statements which are wrong.

a. An articulated lorry is another term for a semi-trailer.
b. Lorry drivers often check up on the EU police.
c. HGV is short for handy goods van.
d. There is a toll for trucks on German motorways.
e. Truck drivers take too many rests.
f. Road transport is getting more expensive.
g. More goods are carried by rail than by road in Europe.
h. More freight is sent by rail in the USA than in the EU.
i. A lot of goods are transported on the British inland waterways.
j. Freight in Europe is increasingly being transported on the inland waterways.

Activity

Rail freight

Task 8

Use the internet to find out all you can about one of the following items. Then write a short description of each item (between 15 and 30 words).

- Hopper cars
- Double-stack cars
- Liquid bulk cargo
- Tank containers

Grammar

Must, need or have to?

Take care with the negative forms of "must":
I must go. = Ich muss gehen.   **but**   I must not go. = Ich darf nicht gehen.
He has to go. = Er muss gehen.   **but**   He doesn't have to go. = Er muss nicht gehen.

Must is an incomplete verb: the missing forms (Past Tense, Present Perfect, Past Perfect, Future) are replaced with the verbs "need" or "have to".
I must go today. – I had to go yesterday. – I will have to go tomorrow.

Task 9

Put the correct form of "must", "need" or "have to" into the gaps in the following sentences.

a. You …(1)… always stop when the traffic light is red.
b. Please be careful! You …(2)… spill coffee over the customs forms.
c. You …(3)… send it by air, because we are not in a hurry. You can send it by sea.
d. I …(4)… finish this report because the boss wants it this afternoon.
e. Lovely, it is Sunday morning. I …(5)… get up early!
f. When you have had some drinks, you …(6)… drive your car.
g. You …(7)… have an HGV licence to drive a heavy goods vehicle.
h. You …(8)… pay VAT on goods from outside the EU.

Listening

A quote for a transport job

Task 10

Listen to track 7, then answer the questions below.

a. What is the name of the freight forwarder who answers the phone?
b. What is the customer's name?

c. Which company does he work for?
d. What does he want?
e. Why doesn't he get a quote online?
f. What commodity does he want to send?
g. What is the quantity?
h. Which country is the consignment destined for?
i. Write down the name and address of the consignee.
j. When must the goods be delivered?

Vocabulary trainer

Task 11

American English is often different from British English – although the differences have become fewer in the last decade, with more international communication through new media. Find the pairs of terms which refer to the same thing.

British English	American English
hopper wagon	highway
motorway	freight train
articulated lorry	large truck
HGV	hauler / haulage company
goods train	railroad
railway	hopper car
haulier	semi-trailer

Grammar

The Past Tense and the Present Perfect

Use the Simple Past/Past Tense ("walked", "saw") <u>when a past time is given</u>, so it is clear that the activity is finished, for example: *I went to Paris last year.*
Key expressions for the Past Tense are: yesterday, last week, last year, in 1989, two days ago, in the past, when I was a child, when.

Use the Present Perfect <u>when no past time is given</u>, for example: *I have been to Paris.*
Key expressions for the Present Perfect are: already, yet, just, ever, never.

Task 12

Explain the difference between the following pairs of sentences:

a. Charlie Chaplin made a lot of films. – Madonna has made some films.
b. Shakespeare wrote a lot of plays. – J. K. Rowling has written a lot of books.
c. My grandmother never went to the USA. – I have never visited New York.

Task 13

Which sentence is correct?

a. Have you seen see the new film yet? – Did you see the new film yet?
b. Where have you worked last year? – Where did you work last year?
c. My brother has travelled to twenty concerts so far – My brother travelled to twenty concerts so far.
d. I have never played tennis. – I never played tennis.
e. I have learned English when I was at school. – I learned English when I was at school.
f. My friend has already read the new book. – My friend already read the new book.
g. Have you ever written a really long letter? – Did you ever write a really long letter?
h. How many SMS have you sent yesterday? – How many SMS did you send yesterday?

Thirty years in the road-transport business

My name is Emma Jones. I have worked for Swan Transport for thirty years and I have seen a lot of changes. Swan Transport Ltd started as a small local haulage business in 1954, but since then it has changed its name to the Swan Logistics Group and has set up a network covering most of Western Europe. But it is not just that our company has expanded. The whole job of freight forwarding has changed. The quantity of goods that are imported and exported has increased, for one thing, and so have the demands and expectations of customers. Everything has become bigger and faster: the roads, the vehicle fleet, connections to mainland Europe and international communications and transactions.

Thirty years ago it took at least three and a half hours for a lorry to get from Dover to Calais on the ferry. Now it takes 45 minutes through the Channel Tunnel. My husband is an HGV driver for Swan, and he says it all goes faster, but that doesn't mean less work for the drivers. On the contrary, he is under more time-pressure than he was before.

I am an office worker and my daily tasks have changed, too. When I started as assistant to the manager, I spent most of my time typing letters. Developments in IT have changed all that. Today, most communication is by e-mail, if not on the phone or online. We send out bills and reminders by post, but they are generated by the computer system and all we have to do is print them. We even print the stamps on

the envelopes. I have had to learn to use computers, of course. At first it was difficult, but our new software makes it possible to work much faster and more efficiently.

25 When a customer makes an enquiry about a routine transport job, all I have to do is enter the details into the program, and it automatically calculates the distance and times and costs. If the order is confirmed, then the software automatically allocates a vehicle and any necessary loading aids, like pallets or fork-lift trucks. It also prepares all necessary documents, such as the road waybill and the manifest (this is the cargo list). When the
30 goods are in transit, the barcodes are scanned at each point on the journey, so that the customer can track and trace his consignment on-line. And when the job is completed, an invoice is sent automatically. But as my husband says, all this new technology does not mean less work for us. It just means we can give a better service.

Comprehension

Task 14

Read the text "Thirty years in the road-transport business" and answer the questions.

a. How long has Emma worked for Swan Transport?
b. When did the company start?
c. In what ways has the company changed?
d. What has happened to the vehicle fleet?
e. How long did the Channel crossing take 30 years ago?
f. What is Emma's husband's job?
g. What does Emma do?
h. Why has her job changed since she started?
i. Does she type many letters now?
j. List some of the tasks that have now become automated.
k. List at least two loading aids.
l. How can a customer find out exactly where his goods are when they are in transit?

Vocabulary trainer

Definitions

Task 15

Find the definition of each term.

A manifest …	… is a transport document needed for road transport.
A road waybill …	… is a branch of technology which is concerned with the exchange of information.
A loading aid …	… is a list of all the goods that make up the consignment.
A haulage business …	… is a set of goods for transport and delivery.
A vehicle fleet …	… is the set of vans, lorries and other vehicles used by the company.
IT …	… is a thing (a tool, for example or a type of packaging) needed to load the goods.
A consignment …	… is a company that specialises in transporting goods by road.

Business Tip!

Writing e-mails

The subject line

Do not forget to write one.

The salutation

"Hi" or "Good morning" or "Hello" are OK for business e-mails (although not for business letters). You can also begin an e-mail with "Dear …".

The body of the communication

In an e-mail to someone you know, "See you Thurs. pm" is OK but in a letter or an e-mail to a new customer it is better to write: " I look forward to seeing you next Thursday afternoon". Some "funny" acronyms should not be used in business e-mails, such as "BCNU" = Be seeing you, or "B4 U go" = before you go.

Attached files

Always send a short e-mail message when you send a file.

Close

You can end a letter or an e-mail with "Best wishes" or "Best regards". The forms "Yours sincerely" or "Truly yours" are still used at the end of a formal letter, but do not fit to e-mails.

Activity

Frequently used sentences in e-mails

Task 16

Translate the following sentences into German.

a. I am sending you the offer as an attached file.
b. Please find the information you requested attached.
c. Thank you for your e-mail with the requested information.
d. Can we meet next week on Monday? I am free at 11:00 am.
e. Have you received my e-mail of (*date*)? In case not, I have attached a copy. Please reply as soon as possible.
f. I cannot read the file you mailed to me yesterday. Could you please send it again in PDF format/compressed?
g. Mr/Ms (*Name 1*) will be on holiday until (*date*). In urgent cases, please contact (*Name 2*) at (*e-mail address*).
h. Please send your suggestions to (*e-mail address*) by (*date*).

Writing e-mails

Task 17

Write the subject lines and texts of the following e-mails in English.

a. Bestätigen Sie den Empfang eines Angebots.
b. Schicken Sie Verkaufsdaten im Anhang: Schlagen Sie ein Datum für ein Meeting vor, um die Daten zu diskutieren.
c. Sie können ein Dokument im Anhang nicht lesen. Schlagen Sie eine Lösung vor.

Regulations for HGVs in the EU

There are strict regulations for lorries on European roads, to limit traffic or its costs. Here are some of them:

1 Driving hours limits

Tachographs have been used to record driving hours since 1952. Today's digital tachographs are more difficult to tamper with than earlier ones. All commercial vehicles over 7.5 tons in the EU have to have a digital tachograph. The number of hours that a driver is allowed to drive his vehicle is regulated by European law. The law also says how many breaks he must take, and for how long (for example, 45 minutes rest-time after four and a half hours of driving). These rules ensure that drivers do not have accidents because they are tired.

Tolls

In Germany the toll for goods vehicles over 12 tons is based on the distance driven on motorways (Autobahnen). Vehicles which regularly use German roads have an On-Board-Unit (OBU) which automatically logs the toll to be paid to "Toll Collect", through GPS. Drivers can also log-on manually at a toll-station terminal. In other countries, like Switzerland, drivers must pay for a yearly "vignette": the number of kilometers driven is not relevant. More tolls are planned for roads in other EU countries.

Limits on entering cities

As cities become more congested and polluted, there will be stricter controls on vehicles entering them. London, for example, has a Central London congestion zone charge, which must be paid by all vehicles entering a defined area on a working day. The congestion charge is camera-controlled. Many German cities have introduced a limit of a different kind. Cars must carry a sticker showing their level of particle emissions, and only those inside certain limits are allowed to enter defined zones of big cities.

Limits on vehicle emissions

A new directive on exhaust emissions was agreed by the European Parliament in July 2008, and will come into force at the beginning of 2014. It lays down rules for all commercial vehicles over 2,610 kilograms. All new vehicles must comply with these rules, which limit the amount of exhaust gases and particulate matter emitted.

With effect from October 1st, 2013, the CO_2 emissions of all commercial vehicles carrying passengers or goods with either a departure point or destination in France must be declared to French customers (Décret 2011-1336). This applies to all providers of transport services.

Comprehension

Task 18

For each question, choose the correct answer.

a. What does a tachograph do?
- It tells the driver how fast he is driving.
- It helps the driver to rest.
- It keeps a record of how long the driver continues driving.

b. Which freight vehicles have to pay German road tolls (Toll Collect) for using German motorways?
- All commercial vehicles
- Heavy goods vehicles (HGV) over 12 tons
- Loaded semi-trailers

c. How does the "Toll Collect" system function?
- Drivers have to stop and pay at special toll stations when they go on a motorway.
- The system is voluntary.
- The system is satellite-supported: regular users do not need to stop and pay.

d. What is indicated by the red, yellow or green windscreen stickers which vehicles must show in some German cities?
- The amount of particles emitted in the exhaust of the vehicle
- The amount fuel which the vehicle consumes
- The type of driving licence held by the driver

e. According to EU regulations, how often and how long must HGV drivers rest from driving?
- 45 minutes rest-time after four and a half hours of driving.
- Ten minutes break in every two hours.
- Six hours rest after six hours driving.

f. Which vehicles have to pay the congestion charge if they enter the London congestion zone?
- Only commercial vehicles
- All vehicles, whether commercial or privately owned.
- Buses and taxis

Regulations for HGVs in the EU

Activity

Using the inland waterways

Task 19

Use one of the connecting words below to connect the clauses of the sentences below, to complete an argument in favour of using inland waterways.

although · and · because · but · so

Can the rivers and canals of Europe offer a more ecological alternative to road and rail freight?

a. Water transport uses much less fuel …(1)… we can reduce energy consumption.
b. …(2)… motor boats emit exhaust there is much less emission of gases than by cars or lorries.
c. We can plan further use of canals and rivers in Europe …(3)… they are not used to capacity.
d. Canals are not used for freight transport in England, …(4)… there is a canal network which was used at the beginning of the 19th century.
e. The inland waterways in Germany are used, at least for bulk transports, …(5)… they are close to many big towns and industrial areas.
f. The river Rhine is navigable from Basle to Rotterdam, …(6)… you can travel from one city to the other by water, passing by many large and important cities.
g. Waterways offer a cheaper alternative to road transport …(7)… they are cleaner.

Task 20

Formulate some arguments against using inland waterways.
Here are some suggestions in note form:

- River and canal transport is slow.
- Need for transhipment to rail or road.
- Traffic can be stopped because of climate (drought, ice)

Task 21

Hold a group discussion. Should more freight be moved from roads and railways to rivers and canals?

In English, a "canal" is man-made, like the Kiel Canal or the Suez Canal. It is not a natural sea passage, like the "Ärmelkanal", which is the "English Channel".

UNIT 4:
Sea freight

Sea freight rates

1 The rates for sea freight depend on the type of ship and on the type of cargo, as well as on the distance travelled. Tramp ships can offer cheaper rates for conventional (non-unitised or bulk cargo), but cannot compete with container ships. Conference lines (shipping lines with a tariff agreement) have to stick to the price agreement for that particular
5 route.

Conventional cargo freight rates can be by ton weight or measure (WM). Container cargo is invoiced per container (box rate): the box rate can depend on the commodity being carried. Of course, there is an extra charge for carrying reefers (refrigerated containers) or temperature-controlled containers, which have to be plugged into the electricity supply,
10 or for dangerous goods, or containers which cannot be stacked on deck.

Shipping lines always charge for a Full Container Load (FCL). The cost of unloading the containers from the ship is normally included, but for some ports there are additional cargo-handling charges. After delivery to the port of destination, the shipping line is no longer responsible for the goods, unless "intermodal rates" have been agreed, including
15 road or rail transport to a destination address. The following factors are included in the calculation: the distance and the route (risks involved, canal dues etc.), the value of the goods and any storage requirements and finally the operating costs of the ship.

The shipping company can add certain surcharges to their invoice, for example if the currency rate changes, if oil prices go up, if there is a foreseeable delay at the port of
20 destination, or if the transport takes place in winter and ice has to be broken.

Sea freight rates

Comprehension

Task 1

Answer the following questions about the text "sea freight rates".

a. What kind of freight is carried by tramp ships?
b. What is the advantage of using a tramp ship?
c. The quotation for a sea freight consignment reads: "US$232.00 per freight ton weight or measure". Is it for bulk cargo or for containerised cargo?
d. Does a full container of goods always cost the same amount to transport?
e. What is a "reefer" in this context?
f. Why is there an extra charge for carrying this type of container?
g. What is an FCL?
h. What can "intermodal rates" include?
i. How can the shipping company get their money back if they have to pay more for fuel?
j. Which other price increases can be passed on to the customer?

Activity

Types of merchant ships

Task 2

Work with a partner. Pair each type of ship in A with a brief description from B and give the German translation for the ship-type.

A	B
A RO-RO vessel…	… is a container-ship that can carry up to 1,000 TEU (twenty foot equivalent units = standard containers). All container ships can carry containers both in the slots in the hold and on the flat decks.
A general cargo ship/ tramp ship…	… is a ship designed for carrying wheeled vehicles (cars or trucks) which drive on and off via a stern ramp. These ships are often used as ferries.
A 1st generation container ship…	… is a flat-bottomed boat used for transferring goods from a bigger vessel to the quay, or to another vessel.
A lighter…	… is a boat for carrying bulk cargo on inland waterways.
A barge	… is a ship that carries conventional (non-unitised) cargo, mostly stored in the holds. These ships are often used for coastal traffic.

Task 3

Write out the following definitions and complete them.

a. A 4th generation container ship is a …(1)… which can carry up to 4,000 standard …(2)…, but needs a special berth because of its size.
b. An oil tanker is a merchant ship …(3)… to transport cargos of crude …(4)… or petroleum.

Record-breaking ships

Task 4

Write out the following descriptions of ships, filling in the gaps. To find out the missing facts, look on the internet.

a. The Emma Maersk is a …(1)… belonging to the …(2)… group. She has …(3)… sister ships. She was launched in …(4)…, and at that time she was the biggest ship ever built. She can carry up to …(5)… TEU (TEU is short for … …(6)… … … . This is the size of a standard twenty foot container).
b. The Queen Mary 2 is a cruise ship belonging to the Cunard line. She is one of the biggest passenger ships in the world. She is …(7)… long and she can carry up to …(8)… passengers.
c. Find out the name of the biggest ship in use today.

Business Tip!

In English, ships are referred to as "she", and ship names are nearly all women's names. The letters MS (motor ship) or MV (motor vessel) stand before the name of the ship.

Activity

Calculating times of arrival

It is possible to calculate arrival time (eta = estimated time of arrival) for a journey, given local departure time and journey duration time. Do not forget to include calculation for **European Summer Time** if relevant.

Question: A flight from Dubai to Frankfurt am Main is scheduled to depart at 10:00 hrs (ten hundred hours) local time. The flying time is 7 hrs 40 min. When will it arrive?

Answer: eta Fraport is 10:00 + 7 hrs 40 min − 3 hrs (minus 3 hours because Dubai time is three hours earlier than German time!) = 14:40 hrs.

Sea freight rates

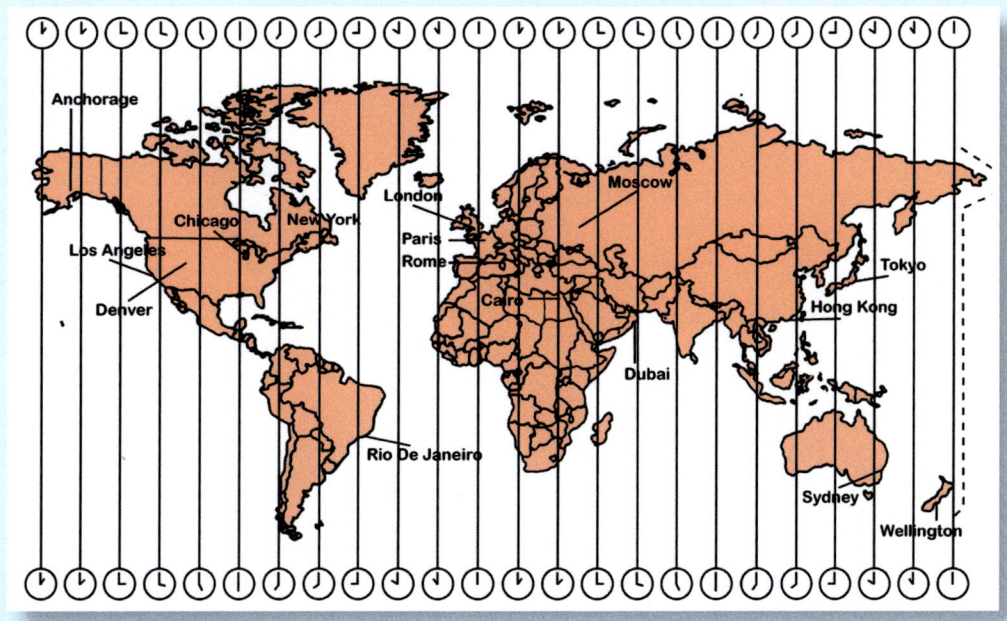

Task 5

Use the Time Zone map: divide into groups, and ask and answer questions like the one above.

Business Tip!

Americans and British people often use the expressions am and pm instead of using the 24-hour clock. "am" stands for the time from midnight to midday, and "pm" is from midday to midnight (10:15 am = 10:15 but 10:15 pm = 22:15). However, when giving departure and arrival times for international transport, use the 24-hour clock.
Examples: Oh six ten = 06:10; eighteen ten = 18:10

Listening

Specifications on the phone

Task 6

Listen to track 8. Write down the information that you hear. Compare with a partner. Listen again. Check your answer (the teacher has the correct answers). If you made mistakes, try to work out why you got it wrong.

Shipping routes

1 If you need to send goods to any port in the world, you will quickly find a ship to take them. If you do not know which ships sail which routes, specialised lists like Lloyd's
5 Loading List will tell you the names and addresses of providers of transport from the UK to any destination. The main shipping routes cross all the oceans and seas. To avoid the long trip round the Cape of Good

10 Hope from the Atlantic to the Indian ocean, ships can pass through the Mediterranean Sea and the Suez Canal into the Red Sea and on into the Gulf and the Indian Ocean. To get to the Pacific from the Atlantic, the Panama Canal provides a short cut, but the two great canals cost a lot in canal dues, and there can be delays in passing through them. Besides, they can only be passed by ships that are neither too wide nor too deep.

15 Huge container ships like the Emma Maersk have special requirements. These include harbour approaches and berths for deep-draught vessels, special loading/unloading equipment, storage and handling facilities, container yards and terminals, road and rail networks, and specially trained staff. If these conditions are not met, the ships cannot enter the ports, so goods must be unloaded, or transhipped, at a large modern port, for carriage
20 to the final destination. In other words, large size deep sea vessels can only dock at specialised ports: feeder services, operating smaller ships and specialised in short sea operations, can carry the (containerised) goods to smaller ports.

Transhipment and on-carriage through feeder services are offered by some container lines to a number of destinations other than the scheduled direct port of call. For example, a
25 container line offering a scheduled service from Felixstowe (South-East England) to Singapore (South-East Asia) would also arrange on-carriage to a number of Far Eastern destinations, if you wanted to trade with Penang or Bangkok, for example.

Whatever your transport requirements, you can be sure to find a provider – or several providers.

Comprehension

Task 7

Read the text and answer the questions below.

a. Where can you find out what ships are sailing to any given destination port?
b. What are the advantages and disadvantages of using the Suez Canal or the Panama Canal?
c. Why can't the biggest container ships dock at some ports?
d. How can goods be transferred to other ports?
e. Find expressions in the text with the same meaning as the following:
  - a regular, timetabled service
  - transfer from one ship to another
  - further transport of goods by another carrier
  - a shipping company that runs container ships
  - the way into the port

Activity

Where is that?

Task 8

Use the internet to find out where and in which country the following destinations are. Write out your answers in one or two full sentences, with as much detail as you can.

- The Cape of Good Hope
- Cape Horn
- The Suez Canal
- The Panama Canal
- Penang
- Bangkok

Grammar

If-sentences

Type 1: a possible or probable condition (it could happen)

If-clause (Simple Present)	Main clause (Will-Future or may/can/might + verb)
If you want good after-sales service,	you will buy our PC with service guarantee.
If you have a problem,	you can ring our service line.

Type 2: an improbable or impossible condition (it is unlikely to happen)

If-clause (Simple Past)	Main clause (would/could/might + verb)
If I didn't have a PC,	I would not be able to work at home.
If I won the lottery,	I could afford to go round the world.

Task 9

Match a consequence in column B to a condition in column A.

A	B
If the ship with all our goods on it sank,	we will be OK, we have got winter tyres.
If the electronic parts get wet,	the fish would go bad.
If the refrigerated container stopped working,	they will not function properly.
Even if I had a jet-plane,	we will miss the connecting train to Paris.
If the train is late,	you will have it tomorrow morning.
If the lorry breaks down,	it will be quicker than going by boat.
If we take the Channel Tunnel,	we must ring for another lorry and move the consignment onto it.
If we stopped for a rest-break,	I would still get there too late.
If I send it off now,	we would not be so tired afterwards.
If it snows,	the insurance would pay.

"If" or "when"?

"If" and "when" can both be translated into German with the word "wenn" but they can mean something quite different in the following type of sentence:
1. **When** he comes, I will go = Sobald er kommt, werde ich gehen. (It is definite that he is coming, and as soon as he does, I will go.)
2. **If** he comes, I will go. = Falls er kommt, werde ich gehen. (I'm not sure if he will come. If he does, then I'll go.)

Task 10

Decide whether "if" or "when" is correct in the following sentences. (In some cases both are possible.)

a. ... the queen of England dies, her son will become king.
b. ... it rains tomorrow, the cricket match will be cancelled.
c. ... the winter is over, the snow will melt and Spring will come.
d. ... I come to London next month, I will visit you.
e. ... you don't stop smoking, you will become ill.
f. ... the managing director signs the contract, we will make a big profit.

Vocabulary trainer

Place names

Task 11

What is the German name for each of the following?

a. The Baltic Sea
b. Munich
c. Milan
d. The English Channel
e. Lake Constance
f. Cologne
g. The Dead Sea

Business Tip!

Place names can be misleading. English people will not understand the term "East Sea", French people do not recognise the "English Channel" and for Americans, Europe is in the Eastern Hemisphere.

Shipping marks

It is very important to mark goods correctly for shipping. The marks can be printed on the packages, boxes or containers, or on adhesive labels. The shipping marks should include an identification mark, the number of packages, weight and dimensions, serial number and port of destination as well as handling information, for example warnings about fragile goods. These marks are necessary instructions for the shipper and handlers. If payment is to be made by letter of credit, the letter of credit should specify what shipping marks are required. It is essential to comply exactly with these requirements, otherwise the bank could refuse payment. For example, if the letter of credit states the shipper is "E. Mueller", a foreign bank could refuse packages labelled "E. Müller". Here is an example of a marked package:

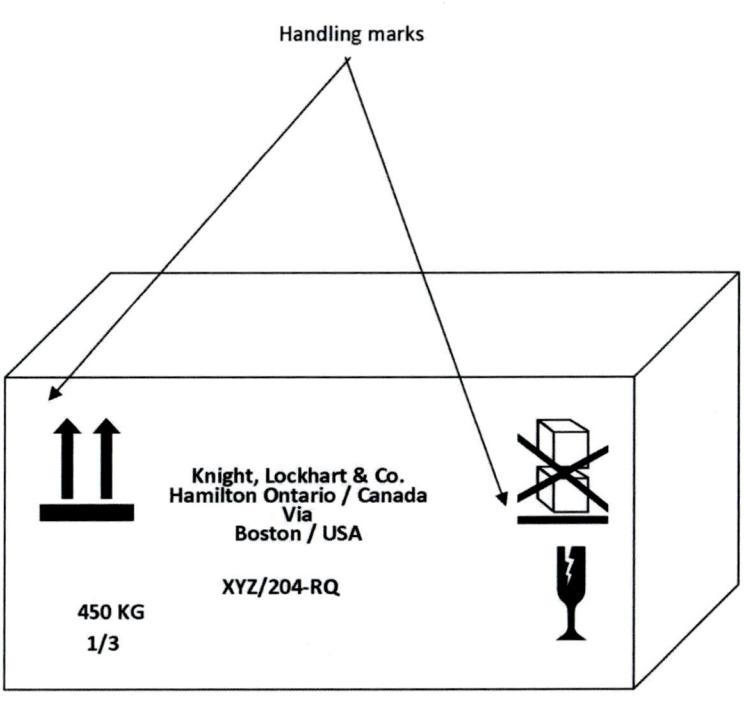

Comprehension

Task 12

Answer the following questions about shipping marks.

a. Must the shipping marks be printed on the actual packages?
b. What is the final destination of this package?
c. Which port is it to be shipped to, before being carried on to the final destination?
d. How much do the goods inside the package weigh?
e. Is the package the right way up? How do you know?
f. Can you stack other packages on top of it? –Why, or why not?

Activity

Documents required for import

Task 13

Electronically or on paper, certain documents are required for imports. The German translations and the explanations in English for the following documents have become mixed up. Write out for each German term the correct English translation and then the explanation of the term in English.

German term	English term	Definition
Konnossement	Commercial invoice	A document which states from which country the goods originate
Akkreditiv	Cargo list/Manifest	An invoice required by Customs in order to establish the value of imported goods
Ursprungszeugnis	Bill of lading (BL)	A detailed list of the items sent
Handelsrechnung	Certificate of origin	A document issued by the carrier to the shipper as a contract of carriage and as a receipt for the cargo
Ladeliste	Letter of credit (LC)	A binding promise by the buyer's bank to pay the seller a certain sum on receipt of goods

Task 14

Bring some copies of documents required for import clearance to your next class. (You can find copies of documents in your textbooks or on the internet.)

IT at the Port of Felixstowe

In the 1980s, the Port of Felixstowe was the first British port to introduce a computerised Customs clearance system. Known as FCPS (The Felixstowe Cargo Processing System), the system is regularly updated in cooperation with HM Revenue and Customs.

The port offers (through EDI, together with online access via the internet and a dedicated network) the possibility for all port-users, shipping lines, agents, freight forwarders and carriers to carry out their business transactions electronically in real time. Information is immediately available to those who need it, without unnecessary paperwork. Users have direct online access to information about containers, bills of lading and so on.

FCPS was started because the volume of cargo handled at Felixstowe expanded so rapidly in the 1980s that it became difficult to keep up with manual documentation procedures.

The Port of Felixstowe also operates a large number of other computer systems which interface with FCPS. These systems cover the positioning of all containers, the berthing of ships and scheduled handling of cargo, and warehouse information. They all contribute to the provision of accurate up-to-date information on cargo passing through the Port, which means higher efficiency and less paperwork. For example, container release to carriers for inland transport can be carried out electronically with paperless transhipment declarations and Customs clearance, thus saving time for both parties.

Comprehension

Task 15

Read the text "IT at the Port of Felixstowe" and then answer the questions.
a. What is the FCPS, and why did it become necessary in the 1980s?
b. Who can use it, and what can they do with it?
c. What are the main advantages of using FCPS?
d. What other computer systems interface with FCPS?
e. Give examples of "paperless transactions".
f. What does HM stand for in " HM Revenue and Customs"?
g. Do you know of similar systems in operation at German ports? Find out by visiting the websites of German ports, and report back to the class.
h. What do you know about the Port of Felixstowe? Visit the website www.port-of-felixstowe.co.uk and find out more. Report back to the class.

Vocabulary trainer

An IT Quiz

Task 16

a)

- a grazer
- a browser
- A program that helps you find things on the Web is …
- a browner
- a reader

b)

- racing
- tacking
- Getting exact current status on where your shipment is, is called …
- bracing
- tracing

c)

- HMV
- UDI
- A set of messages which are exchanged directly from computer to computer is …
- EDI
- EDM

d)

- information and communiction technology
- international container train
- ICT stands for …
- inter-computer techniques
- I can't type

e)

- Wordy Weedy and Weak
- World Wide Wait
- WWW stands for …
- Wonderful World of Web
- World Wide Web

Activity

Shipping dangerous goods by sea

Task 17

Dangerous goods are divided into 9 main categories.

Class 1: Explosives
Class 2: Gases
Class 3: Flammable liquids
Class 4: Other flammables
Class 5: Oxidisers
Class 6: Toxics
Class 7: Radioactive materials
Class 8: Corrosives
Class 9: Miscellaneous

Dangerous goods are not only things like industrial chemicals or military weapons. Place each of the following household items in one (or in some cases, in more than one) of the 9 categories, if they are dangerous, or classify them as "non-dangerous".

How many of the items in the list would be "marine pollutants", that is, would poison the sea water?

a. hair-spray aerosols
b. chocolate bars
c. bleach (hydrogen peroxide)
d. fireworks
e. cigarette-lighter fuel
f. weed killer
g. matches
h. plastic foil
i. medical supplies (pills and medicines)
j. medical supplies (X-ray machine)
k. paint remover
l. shampoo
m. lavatory cleaner
n. whisky

UNIT 5:
Containerisation

An enquiry about container transport

1 Liz Jones: Hello. I wonder if you can help me. I need to arrange to ship some goods to Singapore, and I would like to have an idea of what it would cost.
   Tim Rider: Yes, I'm sure we can help. We regularly arrange shipments to Asian countries. Can you tell me the size and weight of the items?
5 Liz: Well, I'm not sure about the weight. I think they would take up about 20 – 25 cubic metres, that is, when they are packed in packing cases.
   Tim: Could you tell me what is involved? I mean, what goods are you sending?
   Liz: My first export order ever! I make special modern furniture. A store in Singapore wants to exhibit my stuff!
10 Tim: I can't make a firm offer without knowing the weight.
   Liz: Actually, I only want to have a vague idea of the costs.
   Tim: OK. Well, you haven't got an FCL there. However, we offer very good box-rates for FCLs, so it would probably be worthwhile to take FCL rather than LCL.
15 Liz: Sorry, I don't understand you. Could you speak in English words, instead of letters?
   Tim: Oh, sorry. Your consignment would not be a Full Container Load. But it would probably not be less expensive to send it as a Less than Container Load, because the rates for LCLs are higher, and you have to pay a consolida-
20 tion fee – sorry again, that means you would have to pay our consolidation agent to group your load with another one or more loads going to the same destination. It would then be stuffed in a groupage container. Then there is a further fee to break bulk at Singapore, that is, to transfer your consignment and to send it on to its final destination.
25 Liz: So you would advise me to send my consignment FCL?
   Tim: I think so, yes. If you send me an e-mail later with the weight, I can check it out. Can you tell me the approximate value, too? You see, it could make a

	difference to the insurance premium you have to pay, if the goods are sealed in a container all the way from our warehouse to their destination address. And our packers could stuff the container. We have a lot of experience with packing for tropical climate, and so you would not have to worry about heat and damp affecting your goods.
Liz:	Of course I can let you know this afternoon. Can I ring you?
Tim:	Of course. Here is my business card.
Liz:	Thank you so much for your help. I'm so excited about the order!

Comprehension

Task 1

Read the dialogue and answer the questions.

a. Which port does Liz Jones want to send a consignment of goods to?
b. What is the approximate volume of the consignment?
c. What type of goods is she exporting?
d. What do the letters FCL and LCL stand for?
e. What does a consolidation agent do?
f. Why could the insurance be cheaper for a full container load?
g. What special packing is necessary for Singapore?

Activity

The advantages of containers

Task 2

More than 80 % of sea-freight these days is containerised. Why should this be? Discuss whether the following points are advantages or disadvantages (or neither of the two) for the shipper or the carrier.

a. Containers have to be of a standard size (or they cost a lot more to transport).
b. Containers can be stacked on top of each other.
c. Containers can be stacked on the deck of the ship.
d. Goods can be sealed inside a container.
e. The same loading gear can be used for all cargo.
f. Goods cannot be unloaded from the ship manually.
g. Loading and unloading can be completed more quickly.
h. Goods can be stored at the port in the containers. They do not need special warehouses.
i. Containers can be sent on to further destinations by ship, rail or road.
j. It is not possible to see what is inside a container unless you open it.
k. Fewer employees are needed at the docks.
l. Special container ships can carry thousands of tons of goods in containers.

Task 3

Can you add any more advantages or disadvantages of containers?

Task 4

Complete the following sentences using one of the sentences above.

a. Containers are more secure because … .
b. Loading and unloading the ship can be completed more quickly because … .
c. On-transport of full container loads is easier because … .
d. A lot of containers can be loaded on deck because … .

Listening

Container statistics

Task 5

Listen to track 9. Listen again and answer the following questions:

a. When were over 3,900 containerships registered worldwide? Give the month and the year.
b. What happens annually to between 2,000 and 10,000 containers?
c. How big are the containerships that can be operated by a crew of thirteen?
d. What kind of number must every container have on it?
e. How many bananas fit into a standard container?
f. How long would a freight train have to be to carry as much cargo as the biggest container vessels?

Grammar

The passive (present tense)

be + past participle (3rd verb form)

I <u>am</u> – he/she/it <u>is</u> – we/you/they <u>are</u> sent

Use

We use the passive when the action is more important than the person who does it. This is often the case in business or scientific reports. In everyday communication, we more often use the active. When the agent (the person or people who do it) is unimportant, it is not included in the passive sentence.

Active	Passive
The employees pack the goods. (Die Mitarbeiter verpacken die Waren.)	The goods are packed (by the employees). (Die Waren werden (von Mitarbeitern) verpackt.)
People buy computers. (Leute kaufen Rechner.)	Computers are bought (by people). (Rechner werden (von Leuten) gekauft.)

Task 6

Put the following sentences into the passive:

a. A groupage agent consolidates consignments for the same destination port.
b. Employees stuff each container.
c. Drivers drive the trailers to the port.
d. Dockers load the containers onto ships.
e. Dock-workers unload the containers from the ship.
f. Carriers take the Full Container Loads to their destination.
g. Break-bulk agents strip the LCL containers.
h. They separate the different consignments.
i. They repack each individual consignment and send it to its destination.

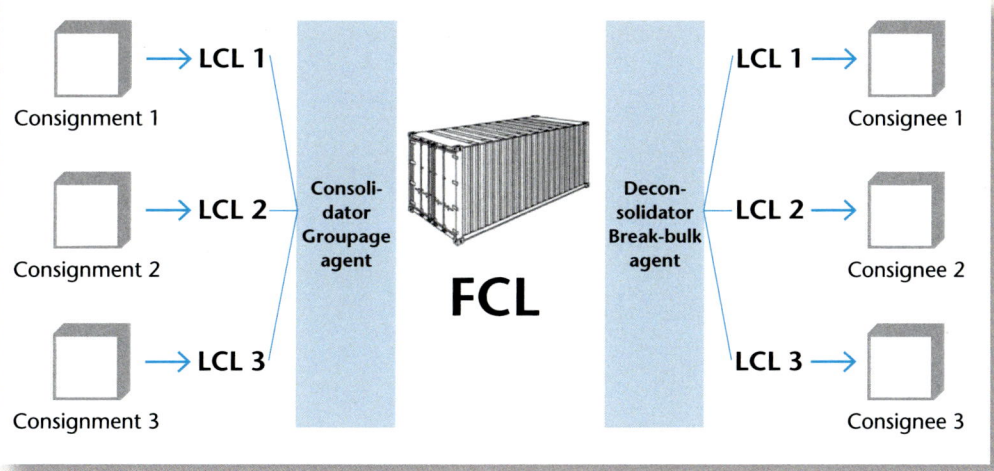

Types of containers

The containers most used for maritime transport are 20-foot- or 40-foot long ISO containers (ISO stands for International Standards Organisation).

As the use of non-standard containers causes loading, stowage and hauling problems, it can be much more expensive to ship containers which do not comply with ISO standards. On a purpose-built container ship, thousands of TEU containers are stowed in the special cells below deck or stacked on deck. Of course this only works if they are of standard size.

The shipper must declare the contents of the containers. Some goods must be stowed below deck and some containers cannot have other containers stacked on top of them. Dangerous goods must be placed on deck, not in the ship. All containers must be sealed once stuffed. This is important, as it is the only way to check that the container has not been opened in transit.

Within the scope of the standard exterior measurements, many different types of container have been developed. The aim is to provide ideal packing space for all kinds of goods. For example, containers designed for transporting fashion items can have hanging

15 rails to hang the garments, insulated containers keep goods at a steady temperature, ventilated containers or refrigerated containers (reefers) can be required for perishable goods, and special high-top or open-top containers allow the transport of high loads. Liquid bulk can be transported in tank-containers, dry bulk in containers with loading hoppers in the roof panel.

Comprehension

Task 7

Which statements are correct? Correct those that are incorrect.

a. Containers used in maritime transport have twenty feet.
b. Shipping lines make customers pay more for carrying non-standard containers.
c. Specially-designed vessels can carry thousands of containers.
d. It makes no difference which containers are stowed below deck or on deck.
e. Containers must be sealed so that they can be properly stuffed.
f. The inside of every container is identical.
g. There are special refrigerated containers for fashion garments.
h. Reefers have different external measurements from standard containers.
i. Liquids like milk or oil are transported in tank containers.

Activity

Giving precise specifications

Task 8

Find the correct nouns for the following adjectives and verbs:

a. wide – width
b. deep – …
c. long – …
d. broad – …
e. thick – …
f. high – …
g. weigh – …

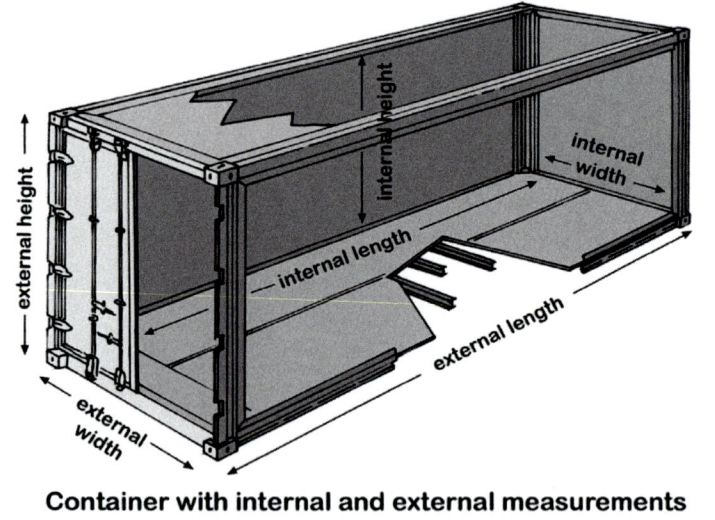

Container with internal and external measurements

Task 9

Why is it necessary to give the external and internal measurements of a container? Discuss this with your partner.

Business Tip!

In North America measures are usually given in feet and inches. In the UK, both metric and imperial measures are used, but the metric system is officially recognised.

1 inch (1") = 2.54 cm	1 foot (1') = 30.48 cm	1 yard (1 yd) = 91.44 cm
1 ounce (1 oz) = 31.1 g	1 pound (1 lb) = 454 g	1 hundredweight (cwt) = 50.8 kg

Take care: 1 (American) short ton = 907 kg; 1 (British) long ton = 1,016 kg

Vocabulary trainer

Task 10

Give the special term for the following:

a. A consignment which fills a whole container
b. A person or company that groups consignments together to fill containers
c. To fill or pack a container with goods
d. To unpack the goods from a container
e. A twenty-foot ISO container
f. A refrigerated container

Container loads of rubber ducks

Container ships can lose containers from their decks in stormy weather – either accidentally or on purpose, to prevent further damage to the ship. If the containers break open, large quantities of goods of all different kinds can end up in the waters of the oceans. There are, unfortunately, huge rafts of plastic rubbish in the sea and on beaches. However, this flotsam can also be of great help to researchers who are charting ocean currents.

In 1990, thousands of Nike shoes fell into the ocean from a container ship, and aroused the interest of oceanographers. Another example is the load of rubber ducks which has been floating round the world since January 1992. The ducks, together with other bath-time toy animals such as fish and frogs in bright colours, were made in China for a US toy company. They are made of durable plastic and were intended to float in children's baths. Since then they have managed to survive storms, winds, currents, heat and cold and have been carried round the world by ocean currents.

On that stormy January night back in 1992, the case containing the ducks landed in the eastern Pacific Ocean. Thousands of definitely-not-natural ducks and other plastic animals started swimming. The oceanographer Curtis Ebbesmeyer was already interested in the movement of flotsam: he had followed the passage of the Nike shoes that fell into the ocean in 1990. The flocks of plastic toys (29,000 was the full consignment) were better for his purpose, because they just do not sink, and they are easy to identify because, although by now they have become bleached white, they still bear the logo of the US toy company: "The First Years."

The plastic toys were caught up in a number of different currents. Some of the ducks went northwards. Ten months later they began to wash up on the coast of Alaska. But they did not only end up there. Some were found in Japan, others in North America, while others got into the frozen waters of the Arctic. In 2000, ducks were found on the North Atlantic coast, from Maine to Massachusetts, and by 2007 they reached the coasts of The United Kingdom. Other groups of ducks were carried southwards, and ended up in Australia or in Africa. If you happen to find a small plastic animal on the beach, with the words "The First Years" printed on it, you know what to do: contact Curtis Ebbesmeyer via the internet!

Comprehension

Task 11

Which of the following statements are correct? Correct those which are incorrect.

a. Container ships can unfortunately end up as plastic rubbish on the beach.
b. A container of bath-toys destined for the US was lost in the Pacific in 1990.
c. The toys were all shaped like yellow ducks.
d. The plastic animals have "US toy company" printed on them.
e. The movement of the plastic toys helps to map ocean currents.
f. All the rubber ducks were carried in the same direction and ended up on the same shore.
g. The toys were washed up on the shores of North America before they reached Europe.

Activity

Find out for yourself!

Task 12

Use an internet search engine to find out more about the rubber ducks and the ocean currents. Either write a short report or make a map showing the movement of the plastic toys.

Grammar

The Passive (all tenses)

Form: be + Past Participle (3rd verb form)

They sent it. – It was sent. (Past Tense)
They have sent it. – It has been sent. (Present Perfect)
They will send it. – It will be sent. (Will-Future)

Task 13

Put the following sentences into the passive (in some sentences, you need to include the "agent"; in others you do not):

a. A ship lost a container of toys in a storm.
b. The stormy waves broke the container.
c. Ocean currents carried the toys all over the world.
d. People have found the toys in America, Japan, the UK and other countries.
e. Oceanographers can use the data to plot the currents of the oceans.
f. The waves are still carrying the little plastic bath toys around the world.
g. Perhaps people will soon find some of the toys on the coasts of Germany.

Activity

E-mail correspondence: goods delivery

Read Ted's e-mail to Bill, sales manager at the British firm Supergaskets, (Hareston Industrial Estate, LH 352 RI Hareston, UK) then do the exercises which follow. Ted is the procurement manager of Glover Motors, 65520, Heinheim, Germany

From: ted.day@glovermotors.de.com
To: bill.bailey@supergskt.uk.com
Cc:
Subject: Our Order 13/452

Hi Bill!

Please arrange for delivery to our plant in Heinheim of 8,000 (= 1 FCL) automobile gaskets, type XYZ123, on Wednesday 12th May between 10:00 and 12:00 am. Confirmation of availability ASAP.

Regards,
Ted

Task 14

Write out the full text of Bill's reply, using the following words:

confirm · delay · pieces · regards · requested · sorry · supply

---

From: bill.bailey@supergskt.uk.com
To: ted.day@glovermotors.de.com
Cc:
Subject: Your order 13/452

Dear Ted,

We can (1) … only 6,000 YXZ123 within the time window (2) … in your e-mail. I'm very (3) … about this, but we have no further stocks in our warehouse. We can dispatch an FCL to Heinheim tomorrow with the 6,000 from stock, but there will be a (4) … of two weeks before we can make up the back-log of two thousand (5) … .

Please (6) … that you want delivery under these conditions.

Best (7) …
Bill

Task 15

Write Ted's reply to Bill. Confirm the order for 6,000 pieces, delivery date May 12th. Back-order to be delivered ASAP. Request a date of delivery.

Listening

A delayed consignment

Task 16

Containerisation has the advantage that goods cannot normally get lost in transit. The containers are sealed, and it is difficult to interfere with them. So when a customer complains that goods are missing from a consignment, there is probably another explanation. Listen to track 10 and answer the questions below. Listen once and take notes. Listen again and answer the questions. Listen a third time and check your answers.

a. What is the full name of the caller?
b. What is the name of the company he works for?
c. In which country is it?
d. What was the name of the shipping line that carried the consignment?
e. Why doesn't the caller know exactly when his consignment arrived in Rotterdam?
f. What was the name of the ship?
g. How many containers were dispatched to Rotterdam for Luxusbad?
h. Were all the contents of the container intended for Luxusbad?
i. Were the documents in order?
j. How many items are missing?
k. What does the forwarder advise the customer to do?

UNIT 6:
Air freight

AWBs and e-AWBs

1   The document required for air freight is the Air Waybill (AWB). This is both a receipt for the goods and the proof of the contract between the shipper (sender of the goods) and the carrier (the airline).

    Because the operation of international air traffic needs the co-operation of a number of
5   states, the content and terms of an Airway Bill are controlled by the IATA (International Air Transport Association). Individual countries or airlines cannot decide to change the form or content of an Air Waybill.

    Air Waybills can be issued by airlines or by their accredited IATA agents. Unlike Bills of Lading, they are not negotiable. In the past, each Air Waybill consisted of a lot of pieces
10 of paper: a set of three originals plus at least 6 copies.

    The new electronic Air Waybill (e-AWB), which has been developed by the international air industry together with IATA, makes things simpler because it removes the need for paper documents. This means lower costs for printing and archiving, more confidentiality and speed and greater efficiency.

15 IATA's target is 100 % use of the e-AWB by the end of 2015.

Comprehension

Task 1

Give the questions one would ask to get these answers.

a. An air waybill is required.
b. The carrier is the airline.
c. They control terms and content of all air waybills.
d. This stands for International Air Transport Association.
e. They can be issued by the airlines or by their accredited IATA agents.
f. No, they are not negotiable.
g. Each one consisted of three originals and at least six copies.
h. The new e AWB can remove the need for paper documents.
i. The advantages are lower costs, more confidentiality and greater speed and efficiency.
j. Their objective is that all carriers and shippers will use the e-AWB by the end of 2015.

Activity

Talking about air freight

Task 2

Discuss which of the following statements about air transport are advantages, disadvantages or neither.

a. It is more expensive to transport cargo by air than by surface transport.
b. Air transport is a lot faster than any other means of transport.
c. Most aeroplanes cannot carry standard 20 ft containers.
d. Goods have to be transported to and from the airports.
e. Heavy or bulky objects cannot normally be transported by air, or only at very high cost.
f. Most airports are in or near big cities.
g. Air transport is considered safe and secure.
h. Perishable goods can be transported swiftly by air.
i. If you want to send goods by air, you normally have to go through a consolidating agent, who arranges space on the plane for your cargo.

Task 3

Can you think of any further advantages or disadvantages of air freight?

Task 4

Which of the following cargos would need to be shipped by air and why, or why not?

a. A pack of daily newspapers from London to New York
b. A box of books from Paris to London
c. Fresh fish from Vietnam to Paris
d. A cargo of bananas from Israel to Brussels
e. A (large-size) carpet from Istanbul to Hamburg
f. Cut flowers from South America to Frankfurt

Expression Bank

I think that it is an advantage to be able to …
In my opinion, the most important thing is …
It depends on the type of cargo, but …
There are extra costs because …
Yes, that is true, but …

The biggest "fishing port" in Germany

It sounds like a joke, but it is true: Frankfurt am Main airport is the biggest "fishing port" in Germany. It handles more fish than Bremen, Hamburg or Rostock, although it is many hundreds of kilometres from the sea.

In the Perishable Centre, a specialised warehousing, handling and processing facility with an area of more than 9,000 square meters, thousands of tons of fish from all over the world are handled and either stored in temperature-controlled rooms or shipped on swiftly to restaurants or specialised shops: in fact over 90 % of the perishable goods leave the centre again within one day.

Fish plays a very important role in the PCF (Perishable Centre Frankfurt) but other perishable goods are also handled here. About 30 % of the goods handled are meat products, but a lot of fresh flowers are also shipped via the PCF as well as exotic fruits and vegetables. All goods are checked for quality on arrival and those that are not good enough are rejected. More than 30 vets control the imports of meat while other experts check the fish and the agricultural products. The PCF is designated as an official port of entry to the EU and has inspectors from all inspection authorities on site. The proportion of goods which are not of acceptable standard is extremely low because air-freight is too expensive to be wasted on anything but the best products. Inside the Centre, strict rules ensure high standards of hygiene: workers wear white overalls and hair-nets. Every two weeks the ice which is used for cooling is controlled by experts in food chemistry and of course the temperature in the storerooms and also the quality of the air is computer-controlled. Some products require temperatures above 0° C: others need to be kept at −24° C.

The PCF has diversified in the last decade and now also deals with pharmaceutical products, for example vaccines. A sharp increase in temperature-controlled air-freight is forecast. There is huge demand for gourmet products from all over the world. To return to the subject of fish, the PCF handles Pangasius fillets from Vietnam, swordfish from the Pacific and salmon, not only from Norway but also from Chile. The fish, fresh from the sea, is flown in in iced containers, mostly in the holds of regular passenger planes, and reaches German customers as fresh as, or even fresher than, locally caught fish. On the other hand fish from Europe, for example salmon from Poland, passes through the PCF before being flown to Florida or New York.

Comprehension

Task 5

Decide which sentences are correct. Correct those that are wrong.

a. More fish is caught in Frankfurt than in Hamburg.
b. PCF stands for Purchasing Centre for Fish.
c. The Perishable Centre is a warehouse which handles only fish.
d. The Perishable Centre in Frankfurt is officially recognised as a place of entry to the EU for a number of food products.
e. All food imports coming to the centre are accepted.
f. All the storerooms are kept below freezing point.
g. The centre only handles imports from outside Europe.
h. The PCF also handles some medical products.

Grammar

Commands and requests

Commands and instructions: Imperative (Befehle und Anweisungen) – The imperative mood

Press the button. – Drücken Sie auf den Knopf./Drück auf den Knopf./Drückt auf den Knopf.
Don't press the button. – Nicht auf den Knopf drücken.

Requests (Bitten)

Imperative + "please": *Please press/don't press the button.*
Could you/would you + base form: *Could you press the button (, please)?*
Would you mind + -ing-form: *Would you mind pressing the button?*

Suggestions (Vorschläge)

You/We could or *should press the button.*
Shall we press the button?
Let's press the button.

Task 6

Translate the following into English.

a. Laden Sie die schweren Packstücke unten.
b. Trocken halten.
c. Vergessen Sie nicht, die Daten zu speichern.
d. Nicht den Stecker rausziehen!
e. Das Gerät nicht ausschalten.
f. Rechts einbiegen.
g. Fahren Sie an der Kirche vorbei.
h. Lass uns die Karte anschauen.
i. Würden Sie ihm bitte etwas ausrichten?
j. Wären Sie so nett, das Fenster zu öffnen?

Task 7

Turn the following commands into polite requests.

a. Open the door.
b. Put it on the top of the pile.
c. Send me the information.
d. Don't forget it.
e. Pass the salt.

Activity

How to load a ULD

Task 8

Read the following notes and instructions. Then place a verb from the following list in each gap in the text. (You must use some verbs twice.)

carry · check · forget · leave · load · make sure · place · secure

Notes

The containers and pallets used for air freight are specially designed to meet the needs of air transport. These are called "unit load devices", that is, ULDs. Because airlines (a.) … a high proportion of air cargo in the holds of passenger planes, the size of the ULDs is limited, and the shape dictated by the form of the hold. Whether it is a pallet or a standard ULD or a refrigerated container, the freight packers must stuff the ULDs correctly and (b.) … them carefully onto the plane, or they can cause danger during flight.

Activity

Instructions

First (c.) ... the whole consignment, before you begin to load the ULD. Sort out any items which are heavy, bulky, difficult to handle or fragile, and take account of these properties when loading.

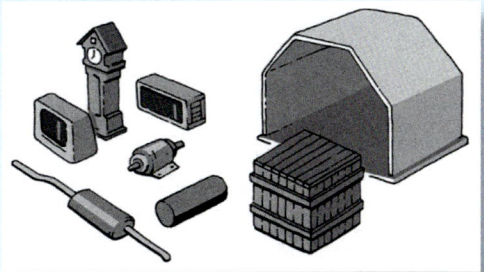

(d.) ... heavy and big items at the bottom with smaller, lighter ones on top.

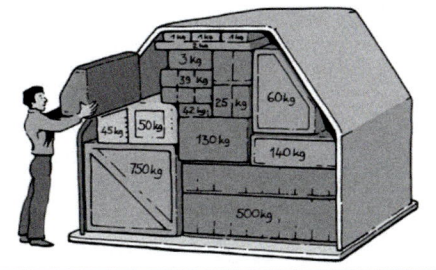

(e.) ... that the weight of the load is evenly spread over the floor of the ULD.
(f.) ... boards under objects which could strain the loading capacity of the base.

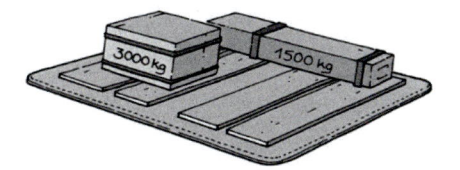

Use all the available space. Do not (g.) ... gaps between packages.

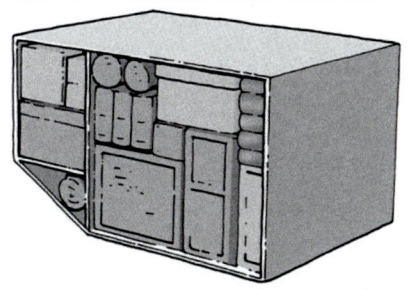

Always (h.)... the fragile or very light items on the top.

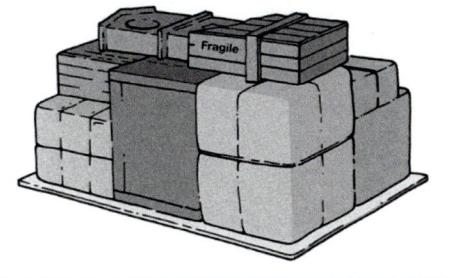

(i.) ... all items so that they cannot fall or move in transit, in order to protect the loading device and its contents from damage.
Do not (j.) ... that an improperly loaded cargo can endanger a flight!

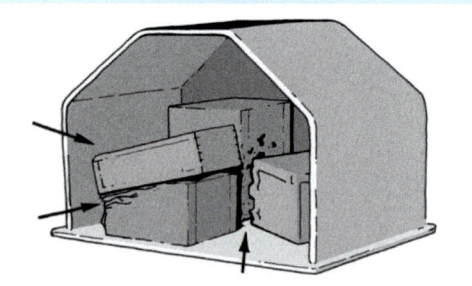

Task 9

Answer the following questions.

a. Explain in your own words what a ULD is.
b. Why is it particularly important to load ULDs carefully?
c. Why should one put boards under small, heavy objects? What could happen if this is not done?

Business Tip!

People often use the initial letters of words instead of saying the whole words: examples here are "PCF" and "ULD". Another type of abbreviation is the acronym, where the initial letters are pronounced like a new word, e. g. "IATA" (the International Air Transport Association). These forms are difficult to understand, and are often only used by "insiders". If you don't understand what is meant, it is very important to ask, as one set of initials can have many meanings: for example "PC" can stand for "Police Constable" or "personal computer"!

Listening

Work-experience with an IATA agent

Task 10

Listen to track 11. Stella is telling you about her experience on an internship (work placement) with a company which deals in air freight.
Listen to the track two or three times, and then complete the answers to the questions. Correct any incorrect statements below.

a. Stella has already completed her university course on forwarding.
b. She worked at Heathrow in her summer holidays.
c. London Heathrow is London's only airport.
d. No other airport in the EU has more passenger traffic passing through it.
e. Stella worked for the International Air Transport Association.
f. She worked in an office where they group small consignments together for shipment.
g. Consolidation is an advantage for the shipper and for the carrier.
h. No, consolidation is more complicated, because each consignment needs a separate house Air Waybill.
i. An IATA cargo agent delivers cargo to the airlines with all the necessary documents for transport.
j. Only the airline can prepare the Air Waybill.
k. Next summer Stella will work in the same department.
l. She will do exactly the same things next summer as this year.

Business Tip!

The word "Praktikum" in German can be translated as "work-experience placement" or as "internship". You may want to apply for an internship with a British or an American company.

Vocabulary trainer

Task 11

Give the full form of the following terms:

a. e-AWB
b. IATA
c. ULD
d. PCF
e. HGV
f. MS
g. ETA

Task 12

Find the words that match the descriptions below. All the words are used in the previous tasks in this unit.

a. The opposite of "consolidation"
b. The initialism for a special container designed to fit into the hold of an aircraft
c. A word with the same meaning as "work placement"
d. A word with the same meaning as "easily breakable"
e. A doctor for animals
f. A word that means "working together"

Activity

International airports

Task 13

Work with a partner.

a. Find out whether your partner has been to any international airport(s). If yes, write a list of the airports he/she has visited.
b. Compare your experiences.
c. Find out which airports have the following IATA codes:
- DXB
- LHR
- JFK
- SYD

Grammar

Prepositions

Task 14

Write out the following report about Frankfurt Airport's Cargo City, filling in the numbered gaps with the correct prepositions from the list below.

by · for · from · in · into · of · to · per

Cargo City Frankfurt is one …(1)… the world's 10 largest cargo hubs.
It is situated …(2)… a catchment area of 200 kilometres of more than 30 million consumers and it is close …(3)… the production facilities of many major international companies. It is optimally connected …(4)… rail, road and air. There are 4,200 direct flights …(5)… the airport …(6)… week and 220 cargo-only flights a week to 85 destinations …(7)… 47 countries.
Cargo City South is divided …(8)… a cargo centre, for receiving and storing cargo, and a forwarding centre, for transfer and distribution. Cargo City South, a purpose-built air-cargo centre, has 130,000 sq.m. of office accommodation, 355,000 m² hall space and 28 aircraft positions. In addition …(9)… general cargo, it provides special facilities …(10)… frozen and temperature-controlled food products, live animals, express freight, air mail and hazardous goods.

Listening

An air freight quote

Task 15

Listen to track 12. Look at the freight quote form and listen to the track again. On a piece of paper, write the information required to fill in fields 1–9.

Freight Quote for Overnight Freight and Same Day Express Service

Place of departure: _____ (1)
Destination: _____ (2)
Shipping date: _____ (3)
Commodity: _____ (4)

Pieces:
   Number of pieces: _____ (5)
   Weight per piece: _____ (6)

Dimensions per piece:
   Length: _____ (7)
   Width: _____ (8)
   Height: _____ (9)

Cargo planes

Transport by air is a vital component of international logistics and trade. All passenger planes can carry a certain amount of cargo. In fact, they always have done, since 1911, when planes began to carry air mail. A Boeing 747–400 can carry up to 150 m³ cargo in the hold as well as 416 passengers in the cabin area. (There is a separate hold, or cargo-storage space, for passenger baggage.) For small, regular deliveries, passenger airlines can offer frequent services. The freight is loaded on special pallets or in special containers. Where more room is needed for freight, the same model of plane can be configured as a combined passenger and cargo plane to carry nearly twice the amount of cargo.

On the other hand, many cargo airlines operate only dedicated cargo planes. The Boeing 747–400, configured as a cargo-only carrier, can carry 736 m³ of cargo. Aircraft designed to carry freight have some characteristics in common, for example high wings to keep the centre of balance low, wide tail-ends and strong, heavy duty landing gear with many wheels to allow landing with heavy loads on less-than-perfect runways. They can also have drive-in tail doors, or offer a nose-loading facility.

Others have wide loading doors in their sides.

For really big payloads, for example military or engineering equipment, a super-transporter is needed. An example of one such plane is the Airbus A 300–600 ST, which is also called "the Beluga" because it looks like a flying whale. The biggest super-transporter – in fact, the biggest aircraft in the world – is the Antonov An-225, which was built to carry the Russian version of the Space Shuttle. This enormous aircraft has a maximum take-off weight (MTOW) of 640,000 kilograms. In 2009, it carried a record cargo-load: a generator weighing 189 tonnes. Naturally, the cost of transport in such a super-transporter is also record-high!

Dangerous goods can be carried by air, even on passenger planes. So long as they have been properly declared, identified, packed and stowed, they can be safely transported. Trained staff are needed to ensure that this is done. However, the greatest danger, apart from terrorist activity, is simply the cargo itself, whatever goods are involved, if it is incorrectly stowed. Cargo holds always have marked positions in them, with maximum weights for this place on the plane. All cargo must be weighed before it is positioned, then it must be locked and strapped into place. The worst thing that can happen is that the cargo moves, and shifts the centre of gravity of the plane. In May 2013 a US cargo plane carrying military vehicles crashed, killing seven crew members. The cause of the crash was not terrorist activity. Soon after take-off the load had shifted, taking the nose of the plane down.

Comprehension

Task 16

Write definitions of the following terms. (The text should make the meanings clear to you, but check on the internet if you are uncertain.)

a. The hold
b. Air mail
c. A dedicated cargo plane
d. A nose-loading facility
e. A super-transporter
f. The MTOW of an aircraft

Task 17

Correct the incorrect statements.

a. Some passenger planes are unable to carry any cargo.
b. Planes have carried cargo since 1911.
c. The Boeing 747-400 can only be used as a passenger plane.
d. A combined passenger and cargo plane has room for a lot of freight as well as passengers.
e. Cargo-only planes have exactly the same design as passenger planes.
f. The Antonov An-225 is a space-craft.
g. You cannot carry dangerous goods on aircraft.
h. Dangerous goods caused a US plane to crash in May 2013.

UNIT 7:
Paperwork

FIATA documents

i.
FIATA stands for the "Fédération Internationale de Transitaires et Assimilés", in English "International Federation of Freight Forwarders Associations". FIATA, founded in 1926, represents about 40,000 forwarding firms in 150 countries.

ii.
The aims of FIATA are to unite and represent the freight forwarding industry worldwide. It improves freight forwarding services by promoting uniform forwarding documents, and also offers advice on vocational training, insurance problems and electronic data interchange.

iii.
FIATA has created a number of uniform standard documents and forms for the use of member organisations. These documents are recognised and trusted worldwide, and so they help in international trade and transport. The negotiable FIATA documents are approved by the ICC (International Chamber of Commerce).

iv.
FIATA documents are freight forwarders' documents and also, for when the forwarder acts as a multi-modal transport operator, multi-modal transport bills of lading (B/Ls).

v.
The national associations of forwarders, such as the DSLV in Germany, can distribute FIATA document forms to their members and keep a register of firms to whom they are sent. In this way the document is a guarantee of standards and is accepted, in the case of negotiable documents, in Letter of Credit (L/C) transactions.

Comprehension

Task 1

Match each heading below to a paragraph i.–v. above.

a. Who can issue a FIATA document?
b. What does FIATA do?
c. Who is FIATA?
d. What is a FIATA document?
e. What kinds of document are they?

Task 2

Answer the following questions.

a. Why are FIATA documents important in world trade?
b. When does a freight forwarder need to issue a B/L?
c. The initials FIATA stand for words in which European language?
d. How many countries have membership of FIATA?
e. Which international authority has approved FIATA documents?

Activity

Filling in a personal Customs Declaration

DEPARTMENT OF THE TREASURY
UNITED STATES CUSTOMS SERVICE

Customs Declaration
19 CFR 122.27, 148.12, 148.13, 148.110, 148.111, 1498; 31 CFR 5316

FORM APPROVED
OMB NO. 1515-0041

Each arriving traveler or responsible family member must provide the following information (only ONE written declaration per family is required):

1. Family **Name**
   First *(Given)*   Middle
2. **Birth date**   Day   Month   Year
3. Number of **Family members** traveling with you
4. (a) U.S. Street **Address** (hotel name/destination)

   (b) City   (c) State
5. **Passport issued by** (country)
6. **Passport number**
7. Country of **Residence**
8. **Countries visited** on this trip prior to U.S. arrival
9. **Airline/Flight No.** or **Vessel Name**
10. The primary purpose of this trip is **business**:   Yes   No
11. I am (We are) bringing
    (a) fruits, plants, food, insects: Yes   No
    (b) meats, animals, animal/wildlife products: Yes   No
    (c) disease agents, cell cultures, snails: Yes   No
    (d) soil or have been on a farm/ranch/pasture: Yes   No
12. I have (We have) been in close proximity of (such as touching or handling) **livestock**:   Yes   No
13. I am (We are) carrying **currency or monetary instruments** over $10,000 U.S. or foreign equivalent: Yes   No
    (see definition of monetary instruments on reverse)
14. I have (We have) **commercial merchandise**:   Yes   No
    (articles for sale, samples used for soliciting orders, or goods that are not considered personal effects)
15. **Residents** — the **total value of all goods,** including commercial merchandise I/we have purchased or acquired abroad, (including gifts for someone else, but not items mailed to the U.S.) and am/are bringing to the U.S. is: $
    Visitors — the **total value of all articles** that will remain in the U.S., including commercial merchandise is: $

Read the instructions on the back of this form. Space is provided to list all the items you must declare.

I HAVE READ THE IMPORTANT INFORMATION ON THE REVERSE SIDE OF THIS FORM AND HAVE MADE A TRUTHFUL DECLARATION.

X _____   _____
(Signature)   Date (day/month/year)

For Official Use Only

Customs Form 6059B (11/02)

Task 3

a. Find out whether your partner has ever filled in a form like this, either for the USA or for another country.
b. Find out the information you would need to fill in questions 1–8 for your partner.
c. Why can't you answer questions 9–15?
d. Find words or phrases on the form which mean the same as the following:
- Christian name
- surname
- your homeland
- the main reason
- farm animals
- presents
- the back of this form
- things sent by post

Types of documents

Task 4

Forwarding documents can be of different types. Work with a partner and make a table with a column for each of the five types of document in a. (below), and fit the forwarding documents from list b. into the table.
Discuss with your partner where each document should go.

a. Types of document:
- commercial
- transport
- insurance
- Customs
- payment

b. Forwarding documents
- air waybill
- multimodal transport bill of lading
- letter of credit (L/C)
- insurance certificate
- commercial invoice
- bill of lading (B/L)
- export declaration
- road waybill

Listening

Do we need paperwork?

Task 5

Listen to track 13, a conversation between Ann Bull and her father John. (Ann has studied logistics and business management and has now joined the family freight forwarding firm.) Listen once, then answer the questions below:

a. Where do Ann and her father have lunch?
b. Who buys the lunch?
c. What does Mr Bull eat and drink?
d. What does Ann want to talk about?
e. What is Ann's father's main objection to her plans?
f. Who wants to end the conversation?

Task 6

Listen to the conversation again and answer the following questions:

a. Has Mr Bull finished reading the business plan?
b. State at least two things which Ann says they need to provide for customers.
c. Who thinks they could save money by cutting down on staff?
d. What is her father's opinion?
e. State two things which Ann says one can do more efficiently on a computer.

A bill of lading

A bill of lading is a negotiable document: this means that the original signed B/L is proof of ownership of the goods. A Liner B/L can be issued by a shipping company and a FIATA multi-modal transport bill of lading (FBL) can be issued by a freight forwarder acting as a multi-modal transport operator.

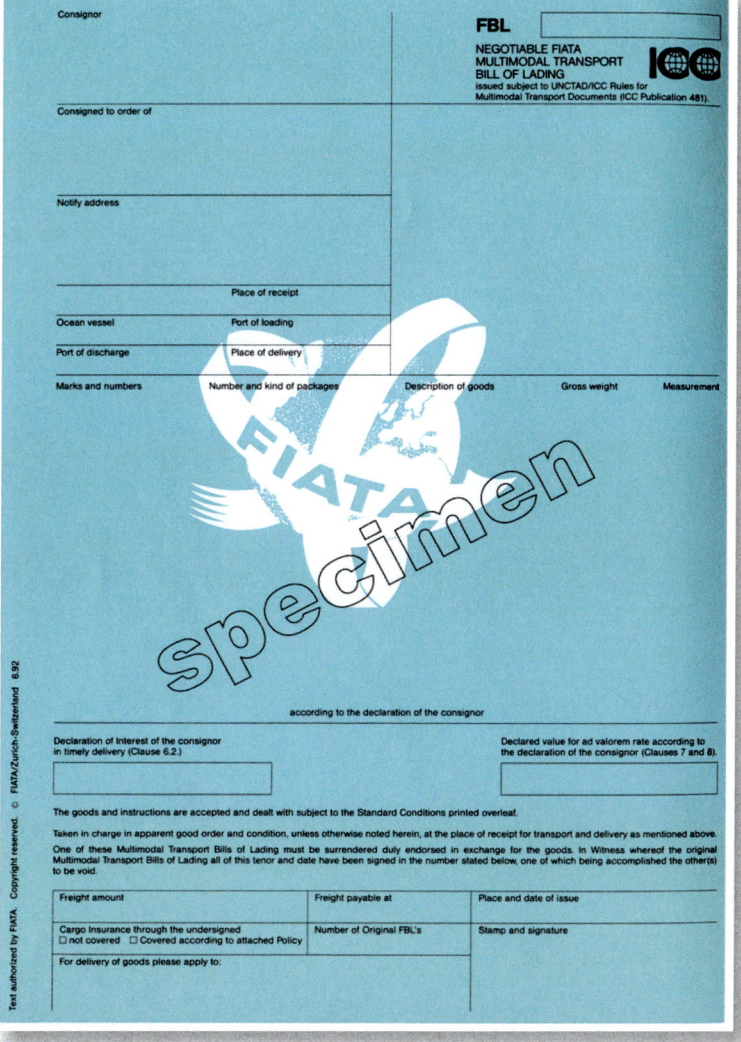

Business Tip!

Take care with the word "bill". A Bill of Lading is a "Konnossement". A duck's bill is an Entenschnabel. But a bill, for an Englishman, is an invoice (Rechnung) whereas for an American, a bill is a banknote (Geldschein).

Comprehension

Task 7

Answer the following questions.

a. What do the letters ICC in the top left-hand corner stand for?
b. Where can you find out the standard conditions on which the goods are accepted?
c. What is the importance of the phrase "taken in charge in good order and condition"?
d. Whose stamp and signature must come at the end?

Vocabulary trainer

Task 8

Translate into German:

a. Consignor
b. Consigned to the order of
c. Notify address
d. Place of receipt
e. Ocean Vessel
f. Port of loading
g. Port of discharge
h. Place of delivery
i. Place and date of issue
j. Stamp
k. Signature

Activity

Filling in a bill of lading

Task 9

Work with a partner. Each partner copies the first half of the FBL form and writes realistic data into each field, down as far as "According to the declaration of the consignor".

After that, sit back to back (no visual contact) and simulate a telephone conversation:
Partner A gives his/her data to partner B, who writes it all down.
Partner B gives his/her data to partner A, who writes it all down.
Compare data. If there are mistakes, try to find out how they happened. How could you improve your technique to give clear instructions on the phone?

A clean B/L

Task 10

In order to get the money from their buyer's bank, sellers need to present a clean bill of lading. If something seems to be wrong with the goods when they are put on the ship, the captain of the ship will have this written into the B/L, so that the carrier cannot be held responsible. The B/L is then "claused" or "dirty".

Which of the following descriptions belong under the title "clean" and which belong under the title "dirty"? Discuss with your partner. What does each entry mean?
a. Inadequate packing
b. In apparent good order and condition
c. Two cases short shipped
d. One drum leaking
e. In external good order

Vocabulary trainer

Task 11

Match a definition from B to each term from A.

A	B
i. Certificate of Origin	a. A standard, non-negotiable consignment note used by road haulier companies.
ii. Insurance certificate	b. A standard consignment note for international rail carriers.
iii. Commercial Invoice	c. A non-negotiable document issued by the airline.
iv. Shipping note	d. A title document issued by the carrier (shipping line or multi-modal transport operator) for sea freight or for containers which will be carried by sea and land.
v. Bill of Lading	e. A document which states in which country the goods were produced. It must be stamped by the Chamber of Commerce of the country.
vi. Air Waybill	f. A non-negotiable document needed when goods for sea freight are brought to the port or picked up by a carrier. It serves to identify the goods.
vii. Road Waybill	g. A short statement saying what risks are covered and by which insurance company.
viii. Rail Waybill	h. A copy of the standard invoice, as for a home sale, but with a statement, usually in the form of an Incoterm, about where responsibility for the goods passes from seller to buyer. This document is needed for export to some countries.

Claiming on transit insurance

Please complete this form fully and return it to:
EuropeanTransport Insurance
Cedric Row
London W1 2BA

We must be informed of your claim as soon as possible and not more than three days after discovery of loss or damage.

Goods-in-Transit   Claim Form

Name of insured *Paul Braun Road Transports Ltd*   Policy Number *H- 451- L. 03*
Address *23, Dock Road   Dover*   Date of payment of last premium *01-03-20..*

Are you registered for VAT purposes?   *yes*

Payment details – please supply us with the following details of your bank account:
Bank Account Name *Paul Braun Road Transports Ltd*   Name and address of bank *HBC Bank High Street
                                                                                  IP 31 29 Ipswich*

Bank Account Number *0094532190*   Bank Branch Code *01235557000*

When were the goods found to be lost or damaged? *11.15 am. Tues 20 March 20..*

Please state exactly the nature of the loss or damage, how and where the loss or damage occurred, and what action was taken afterwards.
Severe water damage to the garments on the front rack caused by a tear in the canvas at the top of the vehicle. Rain entered the container. The damage was noted on unloading at the warehouse and a statement was made by the warehouseman and by the driver.

Where were the goods picked up?   *Mode Bernard, Route de la gare, 33214 Bordeaux, France*
Where were the goods to be delivered?   *Rowe's warehouse, Industrial Estate, CA 34 TH Canterbury England*

If the claim is for damage, where can the goods be inspected? *Rowe's warehouse (see above)*

Please give the following information about the actual goods lost or damaged
Description of goods   *150 summer dresses (linen)*
Value of goods lost or damaged   *1,250.00*
Value of total load   *100,200.00*
Amount of Claim   *1,250.00*

Please state the total value of the whole load (not merely the part lost or damaged)

Important: the original commercial invoice for the goods is required.

I/we declare that all our answers are true and complete. I/we claim for the loss or damage as set out above.

Signature *Paul Braun*   Date *20.03.20..*

Comprehension

Task 12

Read the claims form above and answer the following questions:

a. How soon must the claimant inform the insurance company after goods have been damaged?
b. What kind of company is making the insurance claim?
c. What kind of goods was the vehicle carrying?
d. What happened to the goods?
e. How did this happen?
f. How many of the garments were damaged? (Please state in writing.)
g. When was this noted?
h. Which country did the goods come from?
i. What document must be sent to the insurance company with the claims?

Task 13

What is the English for the following?

a. Beschädigung
b. Versicherungspolice
c. Versicherungsprämie
d. Mehrwertsteuer
e. Bankleitzahl
f. Schadensersatzanspruch
g. Gesamtwert

Grammar

Politically correct language

Being "politically correct" means that you are careful not to offend anybody. Try not to use words which have negative meanings for any group of people; here are just a few examples: Do not refer to "under-developed nations", write about "developing nations". Instead of "lower-class", use the term "working-class". When writing about office personnel, avoid words like "techie". You should also be aware of the way you write about women or people with a different skin colour. In other words, write tactfully.

Some people object if you use language as though you were only speaking to or about men. For example, avoid the word "chairman": it is safer to say "chairperson", or to say "chairman or chairwoman".

Most titles do not say whether the person is a man or woman. "The president of the board of directors" can be male or female.

The problem in English often comes when you need to use a pronoun. For example, many people, particularly women, will find the following sentence annoying, because it seems to say that the team-leader is automatically male: "If you do not get a satisfactory answer from the employee who answers your call, insist on talking to the team-leader. **He** will help you."

How can you avoid the problem? There are a number of possible ways:

- Use both pronouns: **He/She** will help you. **He or she** will help you.
- Use a relative clause: *Insist on talking to the team leader,* **who** *will help you.*
- Put it in the plural: *Insist on talking to team leaders.* **They** *will help you.*
- Use a passive: *She typed the letter. – The letter was typed.*
- Replace "her/his" with "a/the": *The boss runs his business. – The boss runs* **the** *business.*

Task 14

Rewrite the following sentences to make them politically correct:

a. Insist on being served by a qualified salesman.
b. The team leader must know what his team members are doing.
c. The president of the company must put his signature to the contract.
d. The cleaning woman has not done her job properly.
e. I went to see the boss. She was very helpful.
f. I want to find a new warehouse manager. He must have a lot of experience.
g. We are looking for a young man with ambition.
h. A good freight forwarder has excellent contact with his customers.

Vocabulary trainer

Task 15

Fill the gaps in the sentences below, using the following verbs (in the correct tense):

accompany · create · fill in · issue · recognise · sign

The airline can …(1)… an airway bill. The shipper …(2)… it … . A copy of the airway bill must …(3)… the goods in transit.
FIATA has …(4)… a number of transport documents which are internationally …(5)… .
A B/L original is only valid if it is…(6) … by the seller.

Task 16

Give the full forms for:

a. FIATA
b. EDI
c. ICC
d. B/L
e. AWB
f. L/C
g. VAT

Task 17

Give a noun to go with each verb.

a. declare / declaration
b. sign
c. transport
d. export
e. trust
f. recognise
g. create
h. insure
i. negotiate
j. approve

Task 18

Give the opposites.

negotiable	correct	dirty	efficient
good	adequate	fast	internal
approved	recipient	important	seller
import	load	deliver	consignor

Task 19

Give the English translation for:

a. Antragsformular (Versicherungsschaden)
b. Versicherungsprämie
c. Begünstigte(r)
d. Mehrwertsteuer
e. Transitgüter
f. Gesamtwert

Export documents

1. The biggest problem for companies involved in international trade has been the number of bits of paper which are essential in order to carry out an export contract. Information technology can simplify the transfer of data, but it does not reduce the amount of data needed, nor can it replace paper documents, in the case of those documents which iden-
5. tify and accompany goods in transit, or which have a negotiable value.

Why are things so complicated? One reason is that international agreements on transport and trade are very complicated. In order that documents will be understood and accepted worldwide, they must follow set rules. The rules for transport and transport documentation are agreed by international conventions, for example the Warsaw Convention,
10. which sets out the rules for international carriage by air, and decides on the form and content of an Air Waybill. Each type of carriage (sea, air, road and rail) is covered by a similar convention.

Trade rules are even more complicated. Any goods going outside the European Union pass Customs borders. At any Customs Border, specially trained Customs Officers have the
15. important job of controlling what goes into or comes out of their country. They check the goods coming into the country to make sure they follow the rules, for example to see that the correct duty is paid. A shipper who does not follow the Customs regulations can find that this is very expensive, as there are big fines for giving false information or for not giving information.

20. Many documents are needed for export payments. If you send goods a long way to a foreign country, there is a risk that you might not get your money at all. Of course, you could demand cash payment in advance, but then the buyer has the same risk in reverse: having sent the money, he cannot be sure that he will actually receive the goods he has paid for. The way round this problem is to use various forms of documentary collection. This means
25. payment is made once the documents proving correct delivery have been handed over. The safest form of documentary payment is an irrevocable letter of credit (L/C). An L/C is basically a promise from the buyer's bank to pay an agreed sum of money into the exporter's bank, as soon as the buyer's bank has possession of clearly defined documents. The buyer cannot claim possession of the goods unless he has the documents, and cannot
30. have the documents before the bank pays for them. In other words, payment is guaranteed by the buyer's bank. As very big sums of money are often involved, the banks are very fussy about the documents, which must be complete and should not contain any errors. If the L/C states that only a clean B/L will be accepted, then it is no good presenting a dirty B/L or an Air Waybill (although Air Waybills can be accepted in L/C transactions, if the L/C
35. says so). If a name has been spelled wrongly, or goods wrongly described, the bank will not accept the documents and much time can be lost.

Comprehension

Task 20

Answer the following questions:

a. Give two examples of when paper documents are necessary.
b. What is the Warsaw Convention?
c. How many transport conventions are there? From your other courses, can you name any others?

d. Are there any Customs Borders inside the European Union?
e. What do Customs Officers do?
f. Why do exporters often insist on documentary payments?
g. Why don't they just ask for cash in advance?
h. Explain how a Letter of Credit transaction works.
i. Why is it important to get everything right in the documents for an L/C payment?

Grammar

Relative clauses: who, which, where or that?

You can define people or things by using a relative clause, with a relative pronoun referring back to the people or things in the main clause:
- For things, use the relative pronoun "which": *A B/L is a document which is used in shipping.*
- For people, use "who": *The captain is the person who is in charge of the ship.*
- For things or people you can also use "that": *A Customs Officer is a person that controls a Customs Border.*
- For places use "where": *The warehouse is the place where goods are stored.*

Task 21

Copy the sentences and complete the definitions of the following, using "who", "which", "where" or "that".

a. Teachers are people …
b. Computers are machines …
c. Airlines are companies …
d. An air waybill is a document …
e. Football is a game …
f. A port is a place …
g. A truck driver is a person …
h. A ULD is a type of container …
i. Container ships are ships …
j. Freight trains are trains …

UNIT 8:
Warehousing and value-added services

Warehousing then and now

1   Thirty years ago, a warehouse took up a lot of space, because goods were stacked on low racks and picked by workers, either by hand or using a forklift truck. The warehouse manager always knew where to find any specific article, as goods of one kind were placed always on the same shelves or areas. Stock lists were often also kept by hand, the labels
5   on the goods being carefully entered or compared and ticked off on the list.
    Today's warehouses are very different. They still mostly have only one floor, but this can be up to 30 metres high, with high-racking storage for the goods to save ground-space. Racks can be made to store any type of product, from automobile parts to computer chips. In a fully automated system, conveyor belts carry out movements of goods. Once picking
10 is complete, pallets or cartons for customer orders can be automatically marshalled into lanes for dispatch.
    If goods movement is not fully automated, purpose-built high-reach forklift trucks are required which are narrow enough to drive down the aisles between the racks. This happens unless the racks are so built that goods automatically move to the front when the
15 goods in front of them are removed (gravity storage banks). Then there can be a wider picking area at the front.
    The system which makes modern warehousing possible is the barcode. The barcoded label on each item allows each pallet, package or part to be uniquely identified. The barcode reader can transfer the data to a computer system which can record where the item is
20 stored and find it again. But that is not all. The barcode system, coupled with IT, allows tracing and tracking of goods at all times in transit and in storage, and allows real-time records of stock and orders to be available.
    In industries where there is a high profit margin on sales of products, RFID tags may in part replace barcodes. RFID (radio-frequency identification) uses a computerised tag,
25 which can be attached to an object or embedded in it. The clothing industry uses such tags to prevent loss or theft. Costs are considerably higher than the use of barcodes.

Comprehension

Task 1

Read the text and answer the questions below.

a. How did warehouse workers pick goods from the shelves thirty years ago?
b. Who could you ask back then, if you wanted to know where to find something?
c. How do modern warehouses save space?
d. Do warehouse workers go and get the goods from the shelves in modern warehouses?
e. What makes modern warehousing possible?
f. What other advantages does the barcode system offer?
g. What is RFID?

Listening

Workstations in the warehouse

Task 2

Listen to track 14 and correct the statements which are incorrect.

a. Geoff Green is the manager of the production company.
b. You see a lot of people working in the warehouse.
c. A few of the movements of goods inside the warehouse are automated.
d. Anna's job is to write delivery notes.
e. Jo drives a delivery van.
f. Roberto's job is to keep the machinery in working order.
g. Tessa is in charge of software.
h. Jane leads a team of workers in the outgoing goods section.

A liaison meeting

When software needs to be replaced or updated, there are always some problems to be discussed and solved. In the following dialogue Sean Riley and Rajid Singh, two members of the software company Soft Solutions Ltd, are talking about new warehouse systems for the Eurotrans warehouse with Tessa Hughes, the Eurotrans IT expert, and Geoff Green, the warehouse manager. The meeting took place on Thursday March 19th.

1 Tessa: Rajid, you already know Geoff, don't you? Sean, this is our warehouse manager, Geoff Green. Geoff, this is the project leader, Sean Riley.
Now, did you all manage to read my last e-mail? I suggested an agenda for the
5 meeting. I hope you agree with it, Sean.
Sean: Sure, Tessa. That's fine. I've got a few questions on other things, but we can deal with them at the end.
Tessa: OK, can we take point one? The selection of new barcode readers.

	Geoff:	Yes, for me it is a must that the new equipment should comply with international barcode standards. We send packages worldwide, and our customers expect constant tracking and tracing.
	Rajid:	Of course the equipment must be modern enough to comply with international standards, Geoff. Our main concern was to avoid problems between the new computerised systems and the old barcodes, but …
	Sean:	But of course, now we have the go-ahead to get equipment, you and Rajid should work together to recommend the most suitable equipment. How soon could you do that?
	Rajid:	We could agree on that today, couldn't we, Geoff?
	Geoff:	Yes, I suppose so, if you agree on the need for up-to-date technology.
	Sean:	So we can count on a firm recommendation agreed by both of you by tomorrow, right? Good.
	Tessa:	That's great. Then we can go straight on to point number two. Warehouse organisation. Geoff, what do you suggest we do to show it to Rajid?
	Geoff:	I can take you round, Rajid, if you like, and show you how the goods-in and goods-out are managed now.
	Rajid:	Fine, can we do that today, too?
	Geoff:	Yes, if you don't mind me dealing with some of our deliveries at the same time.
	Rajid:	No problem. And you can point out all these "loading aids" we need to list in the program.
	Tessa:	Well, so the organisation of the warehouse can be demonstrated today too? Wonderful. Next point: our requirements. Geoff has a list of "must haves" and "nice to haves".
	Geoff:	Yes, there are many things we must have if we are to be competitive, and offer our customers the best possible service.
	Sean:	Have you got a list?
	Geoff:	Yes, here.
	Sean:	Can we have a copy, and Rajid and I will go through it? We'll come back to you by the end of next week with our solutions.
	Rajid:	And if we have any questions, we'll contact you before that, Geoff. Look, as far as I can see, that was the last point on your agenda, Tessa. Time is rather short, so I suggest that Geoff and I get down to the warehouse and start looking at how it works.
	Sean:	OK Rajid. Good idea. I need to clear some points about testing and documentation with Tessa, but they do not concern you at this stage.

Task 3

Read the dialogue above and listen to track 15. Then answer the questions.

a. Did Sean and Geoff know each other before the meeting?
b. Who was present at the meeting?
c. Who wrote an agenda for the meeting?
d. What is point one on the agenda?
e. What is the most important thing for Geoff?
f. What is Rajid concerned about?
g. When can a firm recommendation be agreed for the new equipment?
h. What is the second item to be discussed?
i. Who will show Rajid round the warehouse, and when?
j. What is point three on the agenda?
k. What do the participants do after the meeting?

Activity

Reporting on a meeting

Task 4

Copy this incomplete report of the informal meeting into your notebook and complete it as far as you can. Use the information fom "A liaison meeting" (track 15).

Report of a liaison meeting between .... and .... on ....

Present:

1) Selection of ....   action   a firm recommendation
                                 people responsible   RS and ....
                                 to be completed by 29th

2) Warehouse organisation action   visit to warehouse by ...,
                                                     conducted by ...
                           completed   March 19th

3) Eurotrans' requirements GG handed over a copy of Eurotrans' ....
                            to .... and ....
                            action   RS and .... will present their

                            to be completed by   ......

Business Tip!

If you are asked to write a report or the minutes of a meeting, do not write down everything people say. Take notes at the meeting, but in the minutes include only the decisions taken. Write a minute for each point on the agenda, and check that the leader or chairperson agrees with your version. (In the report above, the headings on the left were copied from the agenda). It is much easier than many people think!

Grammar

Present Perfect Continuous

Use the Present Perfect Continuous for an incomplete action or for a state which began in the past and continues into the present, for example:
Sorry, my hands are dirty, I <u>have been cleaning</u> the car.
<u>He has been waiting</u> for the bus for two hours.

Use either the Present Perfect or the Present Perfect Continuous for an incomplete action with verbs like "live" and "work" (verbs for long-term activities), for example:
He has worked here for 20 years. (Er arbeitet hier seit 20 Jahren.)
He has been working here for 20 years. (Er arbeitet hier schon seit 20 Jahren.)

For a recent (short term) activity, the two tenses give different meanings:
Present Perfect Progressive: *I have been painting the house.* (It is not finished.)
Present Perfect: *I have painted the house.* (It is finished.)

"Since" or "for"?

"Since" is used for the starting point, "for" for the length of time.
Example: *I have lived here for ten years. I have lived here since 1999.*

Task 5

Answer the following questions using the Present Perfect Continuous.

a. How long have you been learning English?
b. How long have you been sitting in this room?
c. How long have your English teachers been teaching you about the Present Perfect?
d. Have you been looking at your watch during the last lesson?
e. You look very tired. Have you been working very hard?

Task 6

Write two or more sentences about yourself, using "since" and "for".

Task 7

Which word, "since" or "for", is missing from the following sentences?

a. We haven't seen him … the week before last.
b. She has lived in the same house … 1950.
c. They haven't bought a new car … six years now!
d. Have you been to a party … that big one last week?
e. He hasn't been to the cinema … 1995.
f. I have only had this printer … three weeks, and now the price would be half!
g. My friend has been playing that game … eight hours! I think he is crazy.
h. We have been sitting in this meeting … nine o'clock. We have been here … five hours!

The warehouse from hell

Back in the 1980s, a British book-distributor decided to automate its warehousing system. The company were willing to pay top prices for the newest electronic system. Every aspect of hardware, software and interface was tested before they went live: but when you are the first to use a product or a new idea, things can always go wrong. And they did.

The company was so confident in the new technology that it did not make sure that a return to the old system would be possible, if necessary. It did not computerise the processes gradually, module by module: it started the entire new computerised system of warehouse management at one time. This was a mistake: it is better to do things step by step and with great care, because if you get it wrong, it can cost a lot of time and money to put it right.

Soon after the systems went live, there were reports of late orders, cancelled orders and wrong deliveries. How could this happen? The new system allocated positions for all the books electronically and produced computerised tickets which recorded when any books were sold, replaced or moved.

The system worked perfectly on the trial run, but when it went live things went wrong. One problem was that the staff didn't always put books in exactly the right place, or take the copy of the book that was specified by the computer. When the workers did everything by hand, it didn't matter if they took a precise book or the similar copy next to it. With the computerised system, every slight variation caused chaos because once the wrong pallets had been picked the electronic map was incorrect and the required books could not be found. The computer system said some books were in stock when they had been sent out to customers, and at the same time it said other books were out of stock when they were in the warehouse all the time.

The problems were made worse when the staff tried to "put things right" by taking books out of the warehouse without going through the new system. They were doing their best to satisfy customers, but the result was worse chaos. After several months, the computers lost track of where books were, so books which were on the shelves were said to be out of stock.

At the same time, the system started to reject correct orders of out-going goods. This was caused by that part of the program which was designed to check consignments. Each set of ordered books was weighed and the weight was checked against the book-weights entered in the system. The problem is that books lose weight in storage, as the paper dries out. So the computer software rejected consignments although there was nothing wrong with them.

Things went from bad to worse. After a while, not even the most experienced personnel could find the books. One bookshop received six pallets of the same book, another got three empty boxes and another opened a large box which should have contained many different titles to find only one book inside, with the title "Chaos"!

The book distributor lost reputation, customers and money. Putting the system right took years. Nowadays, however, the software works, and an automated system is essential for all distributors.

Comprehension

Task 8

Which of the following statements are right? Correct the ones that are wrong.

a. The text describes the problems of modern automated warehousing.
b. The warehouse stored electronic systems.
c. The story demonstrates that you need to be careful when you introduce a new system.
d. Some of the problems were caused by the staff, who made mistakes.
e. When books had been misplaced, the computer system could not find them again.
f. The warehouse staff made things better by ignoring the system.
g. There was a weight-check built into the system: books were weighed to check they were the right ones.
h. This control worked well because books cannot change in weight.
i. The book deliveries were chaotic.
j. No distributor these days uses an automated warehouse system.

What does a warehouse worker do?

1   Work in a warehouse certainly need not be boring: in modern warehousing many of the boring tasks are done electronically or automatically. The work depends on the type of warehouse you are employed in.

Many warehouses are only for short-term
5   storage. This is true of warehouses run by logistic services providers. The warehousing facility can be used just for overnight storage for goods in transit. For example, goods from all around a large city like Man-
10 chester are brought to a central point, or hub, and then transferred to lorry services which will carry them all over Europe. The opposite is true of in-coming goods. Many transport companies use this type of "hub
15 and spoke" system. Goods are brought to the hub from the points which surround it like the spokes of a wheel. Then they can be transported to further destinations.

In other cases, logistics companies set up special warehouses near a customer's factory, so they can deliver goods "just in time."

The type of work you have to do will also depend on the type of goods you, or your com-
20 pany, deal with. Food products demand high standards of hygiene, and many types of food, such as chocolate or dairy products, need to be kept cool. If they are in transit, they require a "cool chain": this means that they must be kept all the time at a set temperature of around 6° C (six degrees Celsius). Other goods have to be kept at sub-zero temperatures. Ripening fruit needs warmer air, and good ventilation. Other types of product which need
25 special treatment include those classified as "dangerous goods", pharmaceutical products, and cut flowers.

One of the most important jobs in a warehouse is checking incoming goods. Every item (pallet or package) must have a product code or barcode, and these must then be read into the system. This is not only important for the stock-lists or inventories, it means that logistics service customers can know, by using the tracing and tracking offer of the company, exactly at which point on its journey their consignment is. The barcode information is available on a special server which each customer can access and, by entering their consignment number, get the information about exactly where it is.

Many logistics companies offer "value added services". These can include checking, packaging or repackaging goods, package design, labelling, or assembly. These tasks are finished before the goods leave the warehouse.

Comprehension

Task 9

Answer the following questions.

a. Why can work in a warehouse be more interesting now than fifty years ago?
b. Why do logistics companies need short-term warehousing space?
c. What is meant by a "hub and spoke" system?
d. Why would a logistics company set up a warehouse close to a customer's factory?
e. What is a "cool chain"? Name two types of goods which require a cool chain.
f. Why are barcodes important?
g. What "value added services" are often offered by logistic companies?

Vocabulary trainer

Loading aids

Task 10

Match a loading aid to each description.

A pallet…	… is a powered truck used to lift and transport materials, for example in warehouses.
A Europallet…	… is a machine which automatically stacks goods onto a pallet.
A forklift truck…	… is a machine which wraps each full pallet in shrink-foil to prevent loss or damage to the goods on the pallet.
A palletiser…	… is a flat structure made of wood or sometimes plastic and used for transporting goods.
A shrink-wrapper…	… is a pallet of a standard size that can be used in the European pallet pool; that means, it can be exchanged for another standard pallet.

Packaging

Task 11

Match a word to each item in the picture.

crate · carton · drum · barrel · bale · sack · pallet

Activity

A meeting with a customer

Geoff: Hello, good morning Mr Arendson. I hope you didn't have any problems getting here?

Harold: Sorry I'm a bit late, Mr Green. I got to the Eurotrans Head office by 9:00 o'clock, but then I went to the wrong office. I went to room 6 and this is room 9!

Geoff: Can I offer you a coffee, Mr Arendson?

Harold: Yes, please. But please call me Harold.

Geoff: Sure, Harold. I'm Geoff.

Harold: Right, Geoff. I don't take milk or sugar. I'm afraid we don't have much time, as I was so late in coming. Can we get down to work straight away? I sent you a list of the main points I want to discuss.

Geoff: Yes, I've got it here. "Value added service: packaging" – your company, "Natural Beauty Ltd", would like us to extend our services to you. You ask if we can do your packaging for you for the line "Natural Beauty shampoos".

Harold: Yes. We'd like to deliver the shampoo in plastic drums and have it bottled, labeled and packed in boxes.

Geoff: Of course that's possible. But what about the cost of installing a bottling plant and a packaging line?

Harold: We will pay for the plant and all other machinery if your company provides the labour.

Geoff: Well, it is one of the value added services we offer. A lot of companies find that we logistic experts can react more quickly to the market than their factory warehouses can.

Harold: I've brought a file with me, with the details of the bottling and packaging plant that would need to be installed.

Geoff: Fine, great. The thing is, we need to get a decision from the management board as soon as possible. You see, the new warehousing complex will be completed in three months' time and it would be possible to make a separate area for Natural Beauty products, with space for packaging and so on. But we need to plan it now. Can I pass a copy of your file on to the management committee?

Harold: Of course. And can we set up another meeting to discuss it again when you have seen the plans?

Geoff: Yes. I'll try to arrange a meeting in two weeks' time. What is it today? Monday June 1st: so if the management committee agrees to send a representative, we could meet together with him or her at the end of June. Is that OK?

Harold: Yes, that's fine.

Geoff: I'll get back to you within two days to arrange the exact date.

Task 12

Read the dialogue aloud together with a partner and answer the following questions:

a. What are the full names of the two participants in the meeting?
b. What are their initials?
c. Give the time, date and place of the meeting. (All the information is in the dialogue).
d. What is the first point on the agenda?
e. What does GG agree his company could do for Natural Beauty Ltd?
f. What costs would be involved?
g. Which company would pay the costs of installation?
h. What information has HA brought with him?
i. What does GG agree to do with this information?
j. Who will attend the next meeting, and when will this meeting take place?

Small talk

Task 13

Imagine that your partner is an important customer/supplier. You are meeting for the first time. Talk about:

- the journey to the place of meeting.
- the weather (both at the place of meeting and back home).
- previous visits (if any) to this town/country.
- offer/refuse or accept refreshments.

Task 14

Write down at least four questions and answers as examples of "small talk".

Grammar

The Past Continuous

I/he/she/it was sleeping. You/we/they were sleeping.

Use

The Past Continuous, also called the Past Progressive, is used for an action or event which was happening at some time in the past.
What were you doing at eight o'clock yesterday evening? – Eight o'clock? I was watching TV.
In many cases, the action or event is interrupted by a verb in the Simple Past.
I was watching my favourite TV programme when he called. While I was answering the phone, the programme ended.

Task 15

Put the verb into the correct tense: past continuous or simple past.

a. While you (sleep) I made breakfast.
b. She (work) at her computer when the fire alarm went.
c. Someone (steal) my purse while I was shopping.
d. The load got wet while he (drive) to the port.
e. We were driving along the motorway when the car (break down).

Activity

Working in warehousing

Task 16

Describe in your own words what the people in the following pictures are doing, where they are doing it and what they are using.

a.

b.

c.

d.

UNIT 9:
Further logistics services and value added services

Supply chain management

1 Before the second half of the twentieth century, "logistics" was all about military campaigns and how to move troops, supplies and equipment. The word is now used in a different, commercial, sense but the basic meaning remains the same. Logistics is the planning which gets the right goods to the right place at the right time. It is much more
5 than just transporting and warehousing goods, because logistics services must be part of the Supply Chain Management (SCM). SCM is concerned with the total movement of goods through the enterprise: that is, from the procurement of raw materials up to the point of sale. Its purpose is to improve this movement, in order to be able to react quickly and efficiently to market pressures.

10 ### Contract logistics

Contract Logistics is the term used for long-term outsourcing of logistics services under contract. Long-term co-operation between a logistics company and a production company can lead to improvements in the supply chain and in customer relations. Here are some of the services offered:

15 ### Procurement logistics

Cost-effective logistics solutions are essential on the procurement side. Procurement is the purchase and supply of raw materials or parts needed for producing goods and procurement logistics regulates the movement of such materials to the manufacturing site. The purpose of Supply Chain Management is to optimise the supply of materials, which
20 should not be too big because it would take up factory space but must at the same time

not be too small, because that would risk production stoppages. Deliveries should be Just-in-Time, that is, they must be made on demand. The logistics services provider often provides buffer warehousing, to streamline supplies at the factory, and can offer other value-added services for stored goods, such as quality control, repacking or labelling.

Production and distribution logistics

Sometimes a product is further processed at a different site. Production logistics is moving the unfinished goods at the right time to the right place: for example, bringing the required parts to the production line when they are needed. Logistics is also involved in getting the goods from the factory to the store-shelves where the end-users can purchase them. This is sales and distribution logistics. The logistics service provider makes sure that deliveries are made quickly to the stores when they need them. "Efficient Consumer Response" (ECR) is a way to improve the supply to the consumer while reducing costs to the producer and to the retail store. ECR means that the retail store can order goods as and when they are needed, according to customer demand.

Waste disposal and recycling logistics

The fourth link in the supply chain is waste disposal and recycling. An example of recycling is with glass bottles. These can be taken to a washing plant, where they are cleaned, checked and refilled. With plastic or paper, recycling is a bit more complicated.

Comprehension

Task 1

Are the following statements true or false? Correct the false statements.

a. Logistics services providers work for the Army.
b. Supply Chain Management is only concerned with delivering goods to stores.
c. The purpose of Supply Chain Management is to optimise the flow of goods through the manufacturing industry to the customer.
d. Manufacturers need to keep a really big stock of raw materials at the factory.
e. A car manufacturer sends car doors from one factory to the main assembly plant for final assembly. This part of the supply chain is called "production logistics".
f. "Efficient Customer Response" is an answer given by a satisfied customer.
g. Logistics plays a role in recycling.

Task 2

How many of the logistics terms in the text above are used by Germans without translation into the German language?

Supply chain management

Vocabulary trainer

Task 3

Match the descriptions of the logistics services in B to a point in the supply chain in A.

A	B
Procurement logistics	The logistics company employed by a textile manufacturer guarantees delivery of clothes to the boutiques which are the company's customers within one day of order.
Production logistics	The logistics company imports computer chips by air from Taiwan and keeps them in a warehouse near to Buffalo, New York. They deliver each day a specified number of pallets of electronic parts on demand to a leading US manufacturer with a factory in Buffalo.
Distribution and sales logistics	A logistics company carries empty PET bottles back from the supermarkets (after delivering full bottles). The empty bottles are processed into new plastic bottles and refilled.
Waste disposal and recycling logistics	An automotive company produces the car-bodies in one town and the engines in another. The logistics company delivers the engines to the production line "Just-in-Time".

Task 4

In the table above, find the English for:

a. Beschaffungslogistik
b. Verteilung
c. Müll
d. Rohstoff
e. Wiederaufbereitung
f. Einkauf
g. Lagerei
h. auf Abruf
i. Anlage
j. Lieferant
k. Lieferung

Business Tip!

The most-used short-form for "just in time" is JIT. It can also be written jit or j.i.t.

Listening

Just-in-Time

Task 5

Listen to track 16, then decide if the following statements are true or false. Correct the false statements.

a. The Just-in-Time principle dates from 1915.
b. The Japanese car manufacturer Toyota was first to use this system.
c. Just-in-Time means that the factory has to keep a big stock of raw materials.

d. A JIT producer can save money on warehousing and doesn't have to invest his capital in advance stocks of materials for the production line.
e. JIT systems only concern transport systems.
f. It is cheaper for the seller to ship goods in small quantities.
g. Manufacturers require that suppliers and subcontractors deliver on demand.
h. Most suppliers can organise "on-demand" deliveries all over the world with no problem. They do not need any logistics services for this.
i. Just-in-Time systems mean that there are fewer lorries on the roads.

Task 6

Listen to track 16 again. Explain in your own words what the logistics company does for the German manufacturer of packing materials and why.

Activity

Find out about logistic services

Task 7

Visit the website of an international logistic services provider (it can be a German company, or British, or North American, or any country you wish, but the website must have an English language version). Make a list of all the services the company offers.

Task 8

Find out why Bremen and Bremerhaven are important to the German automobile industry. List the services offered by or at Bremerhaven.

Tailor-made logistic solutions

1 Every branch of industry has its own supply-chain needs. The automotive industry needs a flexible and precisely timed supply of parts, so that factories can respond to
5 demand. It would cost too much to keep a big stock of all the parts for all the possible models that customers could order, so the factories depend on their logistics partners to deliver the right parts when they are re-
10 quired.

The pharmaceutical industry needs to be sure of swift delivery of small quantities of drugs. If you go to your pharmacy with a prescription from your doctor, you must be sure to get the right medicine within a short delay if it is not in stock. Producers of food products need to be sure that their products reach the customer in top condition, and that the su-
15 permarket shelves remain stocked with them. Flower shops depend on deliveries of freshly cut flowers, which have to be carried in temperature-controlled vehicles. And so on.

Big international logistics companies can offer all kinds of services for all kinds of goods, but many companies specialise, for example in food products. Even inside one industry every supply chain is different, so every company needs individual solutions to its individual problems. However, experience and expertise can bring the final answers more quickly, both through analysis of the individual supply chain and by use of existing facilities, such as warehouses, transport and IT.

An example of a customised, tailor-made logistics solution can be seen in the agreement between a local logistics company and a UK cider manufacturer. The logistics company now warehouses all the cider products and manages a total distribution solution to the customers. The cider manufacture can concentrate on its core activity. Space which was earlier needed for warehousing can now be used for product development. Many solutions are much more complicated than this one, and involve "buffer" warehousing not only before distribution but also of supplies to the company. (Such a "buffer" or stock of goods kept ready in a warehouse can mean that if there is a problem like a strike, the company can go on producing, or the customers can get their orders delivered). This is not the case in cider-making, as the apples used are all locally grown.

Comprehension

Task 9

Answer the questions about the text:

a. Why do car-manufacturers need to have parts delivered "just-in-time"?
b. Why does the pharmaceutical industry need small deliveries made rapidly to pharmacies?
c. What are two things that a manufacturer of food products could demand of his logistics company?
d. What is required for the transport of cut flowers?
e. Can all logistics companies offer solutions to all types of manufacturer?
f. Why is experience in the logistics industry a big advantage?
g. What does the logistics company do for the cider manufacturer?
h. What is a "buffer" stock?
i. Why doesn't the cider-maker require a buffer-stock of the raw materials for its product?

Vocabulary trainer

Find the words!

Task 10

Read the text "Tailor-made logistics solutions" again and find words or expressions which mean the same as the following:

a. The car-manufacturing industry
b. An inventory or store
c. The companies which organise transport and warehousing for other companies
d. A note from your doctor saying which medicine(s) you need
e. A brief time of waiting
f. Specially designed for the customer

Activity

A real logistic problem

Task 11

These demands were made by a German automotive company in 2005, and met by a German logistics company. What would you suggest as a solution?

- A German automotive company has set up a production plant for cars near Shanghai. They need a logistics company which can deliver the car-doors Just-in-Time and Just-in-Sequence from a German producer to their Chinese plant.
- The time window (the amount of time allowed before or after the specified time of delivery) is ten minutes. If the deliveries are later than ten minutes, the production of cars will be slowed down, and the logistics company will be penalised.
- Deliveries must be made Just-in-Sequence. (This means, at the time needed for production and in the correct order for assembly on the production line.)
- Right-hand-side car doors must be delivered to the right-hand side of the production line, left-hand-side car doors to the other side of the line.
- The doors must be palletised ready for instant use: that is, the order in each pallet must correspond to the type and colour ordered by the company (e.g. ten red doors followed by one blue door followed by ten black metallic doors and so on).
- Each type of door (left- or right-hand side) must be delivered on pallets which can be opened and unpacked from the correct side of the production line.

a. Work with a partner.
b. Look up the geographical position of Shanghai on the internet.
c. Check on the available infrastructure.
d. Find a way to do what the customer wants. Can you rely on sending the goods out from Germany and getting them there on time? What can you set up in China in order to deliver as required?
e. Write a brief report of your solution, in as much detail as possible.
f. Form a group with another pair of students and discuss your solutions.

Grammar

Adverbs and adjectives

Adverbs (of manner) and adjectives

adverb = adjective + -ly
slow – slow**ly**, easy – eas**ily**, possible – poss**ibly**
Exceptions: *hard – hard, fast – fast, late – late, good – well*
Use: An adjective tells us about a noun, for example: *He is a slow worker.* An adverb tells us about a verb and describes in what way or manner an action is performed, for example: *He works slowly.*
N.B.: the verb "to be" goes with an adjective, as it doesn't describe an action. For example: *He is happy.*

Task 12

Decide which form is correct:

a. "Just-in-time" deliveries cannot be delivered (late/lately).
b. It can be done, but not (easy/easily).
c. The whole process must be (good/well/goodly) organised.
d. Information must be exchanged (electronic/electronically).
e. I think we will need to set up a warehouse near the plant very (quick/quickly).
f. Customers expect each problem to be looked at (individual/individually).
g. The manufacturer wants to concentrate (entire/entirely) on his core activities.
h. We provide an (excellent/excellently) service.

Task 13

Fill in the blanks with the correct form:

a. On (fast) … roads, lorries can travel (fast) … and (safe) … .
b. The packing was not (sufficient) … .
c. He worked very (hard) … on the new project.
d. The new employee works (slow) … but (careful) … .
e. Her work is (reliable) … because she checks everything (thorough) … .
f. It is important not to arrive (late) … so please try to arrive (punctual) … .
g. I'm afraid that I speak English rather (bad) … . Oh no, your English is really (good) … .
h. The buyer was (extreme) … annoyed by the (late) … delivery.
i. In a lot of American companies, it is (usual) … to dress (casual) … on Fridays.

Market pressures and "the rag trade"

"The rag trade" is a (colloquial) term for the clothing and fashion industry. This industry makes specific demands on the logistics industry. Firstly, of course, the "ready-to-wear" clothing sector requires specially made containers and lorries which can carry hanging garments. The clothes should arrive at the store "ready to wear" – or ready to be tried on by the customer and sold. This means they must be carried on hangers and protected by plastic foil, to avoid creasing or damage. The vehicles need special rails for the hangers.

More demands on logistics service are made by the requirements of the so-called "Quick Response System". This system was developed in the USA to solve the problems of the clothing retail trade. Fashion chains must offer fashionable, seasonable clothes in as many varieties of colour and size as their customers want. However, this year's fashion will not sell next year, so they will lose a lot of money if they carry too much stock. On the other hand, they will lose custom if they cannot supply what people want.

Unit 9: Further logistics services and value added service

How can these problems be solved? The "Quick Response" (QR) system is a "pull" system which was developed for the textile industry: consumer demand "pulls" production after it. This means that the goods are produced on demand and dispatched within a very short period to the shops which need them. Of course, this demands an efficient supply chain and very good logistics services.

A chain of fashion shops needs quick delivery to stores all over the country or all over Europe. They cannot organise the system themselves. They need experts from the logistics sector.

Comprehension

Task 14

Answer the questions about the text.

a. What is "the rag trade"?
b. Why is it important for some clothes to be transported on hangers?
c. Are all vans and lorries suitable for carrying hanging garments?
d. Why don't clothes stores carry a big stock of all kinds of fashion garments in all sizes?
e. Explain the term "Quick Response System".
f. Why are logistics services important to the fashion industry?

Grammar

Much, many, a lot of

"Much" + uncountable nouns

Much = viel
viel Zeit = much time, viel Butter = much butter

"Many" + countable nouns

Many = viele
viele Male = many times, viele Eier = many eggs

"A lot of" + countable or uncountable nouns

A lot of = viel/viele
a lot of butter, a lot of eggs
"A lot of" often replaces "much" or "many" except in questions (how much/many…?), in negatives (not much/not many), or after an adverb (very much/very many).

Task 15

Which expression ("much", "many", "a lot of") is correct for each numbered gap in the following text?

"Efficient Customer Response" is another system which has been developed to answer some of the …(1)… problems of the modern retail trade. Fast-moving consumer goods, such as household goods, cosmetics, body-care products and foodstuffs, present the following problem: there are very …(2)… different brands, and the customers expect to find their own favourite brand in the supermarket or store. But think how …(3)… money it would cost to keep a large stock of every possible make and size of shampoo! And how …(4)… different makes of soap are there? If a supermarket kept a big stock of all the makes you can get from the shelves, it would need …(5)… storage space – and storage space costs …(6)… money in any city centre.

Efficient Customer Response offers the solution. It involves using cost-effective logistics solutions, which can only be offered by an expert provider. A logistics company can plan and consolidate deliveries and in this way save …(7)… money by making better use of transport capacity. The store manager can keep a lean stock (that means he or she doesn't stock …(8)… of any one product), and rely on speedy delivery when necessary.

Logistics and offshore wind farms

The importance of offshore wind farms in producing energy is increasing, as fossil fuels grow scarcer and more expensive and people become more aware of the need to preserve the environment and reduce carbon dioxide emissions. Wind is a clean, renewable energy source, and since offshore winds maintain higher wind-speeds than onshore, the sea is a good place to set up turbines. In addition, although there are already many onshore wind turbines, the construction of large-size wind farms can raise a lot of local objection, as the turbines spoil the view; besides, the turning blades are noisy and can disturb residents, who may also complain about the risk to birdlife. If the turbines are out at sea, they disturb people less.

Europe is the world leader in offshore wind power. The first wind farm was set up on the coast of Denmark in 1991. By 2011, there were 50 offshore wind farms in Europe and the technology is being adopted worldwide. Since the German government's decision to stop using nuclear power, Germany has been concentrating on renewable energy sources, and especially on offshore wind energy. In setting up and maintaining offshore wind farms, logistics planning is a key factor. Because they can only be set up in fair weather, only the summer months can be used for the installation of the huge turbines. First the enormous parts must be transported to the sites; this requires purpose-built ships with special loading and lifting gear. In the early days of offshore turbines, the machine parts were transported to the ports by road, but because of their size and weight, manufacturers decided to assemble the parts at sea-ports, such as, in Germany, Emden, Rostock and Bremerhaven. Bremerhaven is an ideal location because it has access to a deep-water river and a sea harbour.

The offshore wind farm projects in the North Sea require ports with berths for ships up to 200 metres long and 10 metres deep, as these ships are needed to transport and install the turbines.

The ports also need storage space for the huge, heavy parts, and access both to engineering expertise and to a logistics infrastructure.

Without specialised logistics support and planning, offshore wind farms could not be constructed, and when they are in use, logistics support continues to be essential for repair and maintenance work. The blades of the vast rotors can be up to 100 metres long and are mounted on huge floating or fixed towers. The spinning blades power generators, which must be protected from sea-water and rain. There are many logistics problems to be solved before these giants are in place. A whole new branch of marine logistics is growing with the wind energy industry, and already provides thousands of jobs in coastal areas.

Comprehension

Task 16

Which statements are correct? Correct any statement which is wrong.

a. Wind energy is important to replace diminishing sources of oil and coal.
b. People don't care how much carbon dioxide goes into the earth's atmosphere.
c. Winds are stronger and steadier over the sea than over land.
d. If wind turbines are put up in the countryside, the people who live nearby are happy.
e. The first offshore wind farms were set up on the coasts of America.
f. Germany now has a special reason for wanting to develop renewable energy sources.
g. Wind farms can only be set up in the winter months.
h. Special ships have to be constructed for carrying the whole wind-turbines.
i. Some companies specialise in logistics for wind farms.

Activity

Sources of energy

Task 17

a. Write notes in English about your views on energy sources: should all energy in future come from renewable sources? What sources are there? What about nuclear energy?
b. Hold a group discussion.

UNIT 10:
A job in an English-speaking country

Job advertisements

Personnel Consultants Ltd
Management trainee (Logistic services)
initial salary to £24,000

Our client, a European-based logistics company with branches worldwide, is looking for dynamic, ambitious trainees for future top management jobs. Do you have a degree or diploma in Transport Management, Logistics or a related discipline and at least six months hands-on experience of work in the logistics industry? Then this could be the big chance for you. Successful applicants will need fluent English and the will to learn and work hard at company branches anywhere in the world. If you are interested, ring 0179327812 for more information or send your application with CV to Jill Jones, Personnel Consultants Ltd, PO Box 345 London W1 GI 07.

Comprehension

Task 1

a. What kind of company placed the advertisement?
b. What sort of company will the successful candidate(s) work for?
c. Is the nationality of the applicant important?
d. What professional qualifications are necessary?
e. What experience should applicants have?
f. Does the advertisement say what kind of work the successful applicant will do?
g. What does "initial salary to £24,000" mean?
h. Would you be interested in a job like this? Give reasons for your answer.

Business Tip!

Whether you are applying for a permanent position in a company or for a work-experience placement (internship), you will need to send a CV and an accompanying letter.

Activity

Jobs in logistics

Task 2

Fit each job title to the key responsibilities it involves.

Title	Key responsibilities
Air Freight Sales Executive	Managing the receipt, warehousing, order picking and despatch of all goods in the warehouse, directing warehouse operatives and deciding on operation procedures
Deep Sea Import Operator	Organisation, implementation, testing and documentation of IT projects both in-company and for key customers
International Road Freight Operator	Handling all aspects of sea-freight import documentation, answering customer enquiries and offering flexible service, so as to build up customer relationships
IT project coordinator	Handling all aspects of road-transport documentation, receiving telephone enquiries, giving quotations, arranging consolidation and despatch of orders, while maintaining best relationships with the customers on the one side and the service providers (carriers) on the other.
Warehouse Manager	Building up new customer lists, while attending to the regular customers' needs. The main job is to sell services in the air freight business, to complete monthly sales reports and to provide information about what competitors are doing.

Career objectives

Task 3

Answer the following questions: use the German words for your qualifications, school type, etc. Do not try to translate them.

a. What qualifications do you have? (What German or other examinations have you passed and when did you do them?)
b. Do you have any job-experience? (Have you completed a job-experience placement? If yes, in what industry? For how long? What did you do there?)
c. What is your present occupation? (What are you doing now? Are you working? Are you studying?)
d. Which branch of the logistics industry interests you most? Why?
e. What job(s) would you like to apply for?
f. What do you hope to be doing ten years from now?

When you have finished answering the questions, compare your answers with your partner's.

A Curriculum Vitae

Curriculum Vitae

Name	Paul Wolf	e-mail:	p.wolf@t-online.de
Address	Neugasse 14	Telephone (evenings)	(+49) 6126 1201
	65510 Idstein		

Date of birth	22.07.19..	Place of birth	Frankfurt/Main, Germany
Nationality	German	Marital status	single

School education[1]
- 20..–20.. Idstein Grundschule
- 20..–20.. Pestalozzi Gymnasium, Idstein
- 20.. Abitur (A-level equivalent)[2]

Professional Training
- 20..–20.. Berufsschule Mainz

Qualification
- 20.. Abschluss Speditionskaufmann[2]

Experience
- 20..–20.. Apprentice in the export documentation department at Hartmann Fracht GmbH, Frankfurt
- June–September 20..: worked on a farm in Barton, England

Hobbies
- Captain of the Idstein-Heftrich football team
- Co-trainer of the youth team
- Jogging, training for marathon races

Languages
German (native speaker), English (fluent)

References[3]

Herr J. Müller	Oberstudienrätin P. Stark
Personalabteilungsleiter	Head of Transport Studies
Fracht Hartmann GmbH	Berufsschule Mainz
Aahrstr. 1	Bachweg 51
60195 Bornheim	65207 Mainz

---

[1] *European CVs are written chronologically. North Americans write "resumes" which start with the points most relevant to the job applied for. These days, you can choose how to do it. Your CV is the document that decides if you are invited for a job interview or not, so make it sound as positive as you can.*

[2] *Do not translate qualifications, names or titles into English: leave them in German with a short explanation, e. g. Gymnasium (higher secondary school)/Abitur (A-level equivalent).*

[3] *British and US applicants do not send open testimonials (Zeugnisse) with their CV. They give the names and addresses of two or more people who have agreed to give the new employer relevant information. Note that you should not send a photo with your application if you are applying for a job in Britain: this is considered politically incorrect.*

Activity

A Curriculum Vitae

Task 4

Ask and answer questions about Paul Wolf:

a. When was he …?
b. When did he …?
c. Where did he …?
d. Has he ever …?
e. What does he …?

Task 5

Ask your partner the questions from Task 4 about him-/herself.

Task 6

Write your own CV: Compare your CV with your partner's.

The covering letter

Paul Wolf
Neugasse 14
65510 Idstein
Germany

Ms J. Jones
Personnel Consultants Ltd.
PO Box 345
London W1G107
United Kingdom

July 19th 20..

Subject: Post as Management Trainee (Logistic services)

Dear Ms Jones,

I wish to apply for a post as a management trainee, as advertised in "Forwarding and Logistics" of 12th July. Please find my Curriculum Vitae enclosed. I will be happy to send you copies of my certificates and testimonials on request.

I completed my training as Speditionskaufmann in June this year. This title means that I am a recognised transport management specialist. Ms P. Stark, head of the department of Transport Studies at the Berufsschule in Mainz, will assure you that I was a good student. In addition to my course at the Berufsschule (a specialised technical college) my preparation for the Diploma included a full practical training on the job at Hartmann Fracht GmbH. This is a road haulage company with a number of key industrial and commercial customers.

I am keen to work hard because, as you will see from my hobbies, I enjoy working towards a worthwhile goal. I have now run three marathons, and feel that this proves that I have staying-power. I also greatly enjoy working as part of a team, which is why I am the captain of my football team.

I have been asked to remain with Hartmann Fracht GmbH after the end of my apprenticeship, but I wish to learn more about other aspects of logistics and management.

My period of notice from my present employment is six weeks to the end of the quarter. I will be available for interview at any time in the next few weeks.

Yours sincerely,

Paul Wolf

Business Tip!

The accompanying letter is as important as the CV. If it is badly written or obviously just a copy out of a book, it will not make a good impression. Write about the job you want and why you want it. It makes no difference whether you send your application by e-mail or by post, a covering letter is necessary, and should be brief, relevant, formal and well written!
When writing to a woman use "Ms" as form of address unless she indicates that she wants to be called "Mrs" or "Miss" or another title, e. g. "Dr", "Professor", or "Lady".

Comprehension

Task 7

Answer the questions about Paul's covering letter:

a. How does Paul know who to write to?
b. Does he repeat information from his CV in the letter?
c. How does Paul make it clear that he has the qualities required for management?
d. If you are employed, what is your period of notice if you want to leave your job?
e. How much chance do you think Paul has of being put on the shortlist for the job, and being invited for an interview?

Activity

Writing a covering letter

Task 8

Choose an advertisement for a job (look in newspapers, or on the websites of international companies). Write a covering letter to send with your CV to apply for that job. Include the advertisement, your CV and your covering letter in one folder.

Business Tip!

The dual system of German professional training (Lehrstelle plus Berufsschule) does not have an equivalent in Britain or the US. It is therefore difficult to translate terms like "Lehrstelle", "Berufsschule" or "Praktikum". The term "apprentice" is used only for training for certain trades, like plumber or electrician. "Trainees" usually already have a university degree in their subject (e. g. management trainees). The term "vocational school" does not exist: the nearest would be technical college. The custom of working for a short time as a "Praktikant" is not widespread. "Work placements" are usually only for two or three weeks, and involve 16-year-old school children, who are not given real tasks to perform. So if you want a work placement, explain what you have learned and what you can do!

Listening

Talking about your professional experience

Task 9

Listen to track 17. Pierrette Dubois applied for the same job as Paul Wolf. They were both offered job places as trainees. After listening to the extract from Pierrette's interview, answer the questions.

a. How many interviewers are there?
b. What do the interviewers do?
c. How does the interviewer try to put the candidate at ease?
d. Where does Pierrette come from and how did she travel?
e. Why does Pierrette say it is her first job interview, although she has done jobs before?
f. How many times has she done temporary jobs?
g. What did she do last summer?
h. Where did she study and has she completed her course?
i. When did she take her finals?
j. Does she make a good impression? Give your reasons for your answer.

Activity

Practice for interviews

Task 10

Work with a partner. Read Paul Wolf's CV again and play the roles of Paul and the interviewer(s). Partner A: ask questions about Paul's CV. Partner B: answer in the role of Paul. After four questions, change roles.

Task 11

Ask each other the same questions as in Task 10. Answer for yourself: talk about your own qualifications, experience and ambitions.

Listening

More interviews

Task 12

Listen to track 18. You will hear part of two interviews with applicants for positions as trainees. Listen to the interview with Carl then answer the questions below.

a. Do you think Carl makes a positive impression on the interviewer? Why, or why not?
b. What does Carl say about the things he learned at college?

c. How does he assess his own personality?
d. Would you want to work with him? Why, or why not?
e. What reason does he give for wanting this post?

Task 13

Listen to the second interview on track 18 and answer the questions below.

a. Do you think Anne makes a positive impression on the interviewer? Why, or why not?
b. What does Anne say about the things she learned at college?
c. Would you want to work with her? Why, or why not?
d. What reason does she give for wanting this post?

Activity

Practising for job interviews

Task 14

Listen to the dialogues again and write down some interview questions. How would you answer them if an interviewer asked you?

Task 15

Think of three more questions which could be asked in a job-interview. Ask your partner.

Grammar

Problems with past tenses

Simple Past or Present Perfect?

Simple Past is used with "last year", "yesterday", "in 1992", "when I was a child" and all expressions of past time.
Present Perfect is used with "before", "ever", "never", "already", "yet", "up to now", "so far this year" and all expressions of time which express the idea "up to this moment".
Example: *Have you typed the report yet?* (present perfect) – *Yes, I finished it about an hour ago.* (simple past)

Present Perfect or Present Simple?

Present Simple is only used for activities that take place in the present time.
Present Perfect is used for activities which began in the past and continue until now.
Example: *She works in the sales department now. She has worked there for five years.* (And she still works there.)

The covering letter

Present Perfect or Present Perfect Continuous?

Present Perfect <u>and</u> Present Perfect Continuous are used for activities which began in the past and continue until now.
Present Perfect must be used when the activity has been completed, but is relevant to the present time.
Example: *Somebody has deleted the file.* (The file is no longer on the PC.)
Present Perfect Continuous is used for cases where you want to stress the length of time.
Example: *We have been waiting for an hour.*

Task 16

Each sentence contains a mistake: correct it.

a. I live in Germany since last year.
b. We waited here for hours and there is still no news of our flight.
c. She has been giving up smoking last year.
d. He did not arrive late since he started work here.
e. They have worked here in 1999.
f. Charlie Chaplin has made a lot of films before he died.
g. They have founded the company two years ago.
h. How long do you work here?
i. When I have finished writing the report I sent copies of it to all the directors.
j. We finished the work already.

Activity

Asking and answering questions

Task 17

Find out whether your partner has …

a. … travelled abroad.
b. … worked in a big company.
c. … been to America.
d. … met a famous person.
e. … (Think of at least three more questions.)

Now find out when exactly he/she did this for the first time/last time.

Vocabulary trainer

Task 18

The following verb or adjective + preposition combinations all appear somewhere in the texts in this unit. Put the right preposition into each gap.

for · in · on · to · for · up

a. We specialise …(1)… export documentation.
b. They are trying to build …(2)… a customer list.
c. We must attend …(3)… the problems of our customers.
d. She said she would apply …(4)… the job.
e. They will send it to you …(5)… request.
f. In addition …(6)… the money, I enjoy the challenge.

Task 19

Match the following terms to the definitions below.

situation vacant · testimony · reference · period of notice

a. The length of time that an employee must continue working after telling the employer he or she is going to leave.
b. A statement about an employee's ability, made to a possible future employer.
c. An open letter to any new employer about the employee.
d. A job position which a company wants to fill.

An international management trainee

1 After completing my Bachelor's degree in Transport Studies at Holloway University, I was pleased to be successful in my application for a management trainee place.

5 My training program started in January 2000 with three months intensive training at Seafreight Export at Rotterdam in Holland. The tasks included giving quotations, taking bookings from clients, releasing con-
10 tainers for use, booking space with shipping lines, preparing the documents, clearing the cargo for export and then preparing the invoices.

My next stop, in May of the same year, was Kuala Lumpur (Malaysia), where I joined the
15 sales team at the local branch of the company. The first thing I had to do was to get used to the Malaysian way of life and culture, but this was not a big problem. I had to learn a whole new aspect of the freight forwarding business. My new job was not just to carry out processes of organisation and documentations: now I had to sell my company's ser-

vices. I had to convince potential clients that we could offer the best service. I visited potential clients as a major part of my daily tasks. In the end, the sales team won a lot of new clients for the company.

In July 2000, the last stage of my training program began, this time in the USA, in Dallas. Again, I was concerned with selling the services of the company, but also with maintaining the accounts of key customers. The job is called "key account management". The main responsibility of the key account manager is to look after the important customers and to get new custom. The market is changing all the time, so you have to be flexible and look for new solutions if you don't want your customers to look elsewhere. In 2000, one of the biggest trends was for a larger number of companies in North America and Europe to do business with China.

My main task there was to find ways to fulfil new demands from our existing customers or from new clients. I had to recognise exactly what the customers needed and then find out how the company could use its carriers to fulfil these needs. The most difficult thing at first was to get the price right. I had to put a price on these services, that is, I had to make realistic but attractive quotations. If the price was too high, the customer would go to the competition, but if it was too low we could not make a profit.

All this was a big challenge for me, but it was enjoyable, and I was successful in getting new custom and in maintaining key customer accounts. Now I am looking forward to taking up a more permanent post managing the sales office in Beijing. I am excited about this because it is a new and exciting country for me, and a new, challenging market for the Western world.

Comprehension

Task 20

Read the text, then answer the following questions:

a. What qualification(s) did the trainee have?
b. Where did she start the training program?
c. Did this initial training cover air freight?
d. What aspect of work in a logistics company did he/she learn in Kuala Lumpur?
e. Explain what is meant by "key account management".
f. What did she find the most difficult thing to do?
g. Where will she be working as a permanent company employee?

Advanced reading and exercises

A report about a distribution problem

Terms of reference

Subject: Distribution of Carson's Natural Beauty Products® in the UK

For: The board of directors Carson and Sons Ltd
             12, Green Street
             CB7 83J Cambridge

Date: 12 May 20..

By Michael Carson, Sales Director

Proceedings

UK orders for our products over the last twelve months were analysed, together with the number of trips needed to deliver the goods and the costs involved. For figures, see appendix, tables 1–3.

Findings

Domestic sales have risen by approximately 40 % in the last year as a result of new marketing policies. Four leading supermarket chains as well as several chains of department stores and a large number of individual shops order items from the whole range on a regular basis.

The company's distribution department processes all orders. Goods are stored in a warehouse next to the plant. The warehouse space is already used to full capacity, but the documentation system is slow and order-picking is done manually, often leading to late or wrong deliveries.

Customers expect small, regular deliveries on demand to replenish shelf-stock immediately after sales. The present system cannot satisfy the demand for flexible supply. It is also already used to capacity.

The road-transport company makes runs at fixed times, but deliveries to any one customer never make up a full-load and in some cases only one or two specific items are required. Return runs from the stores are empty, unless the haulier can find return load, in which case our costs are only slightly reduced.

Conclusions

The analysis showed that distribution costs are too high because loading-capacity is being under-used. At the same time, customers are not receiving an efficient level of response.

Recommendation

Our logistics should be outsourced. A specialised logistics company could provide a better and more flexible service for our customers at lower costs because they have the necessary IT systems, the know-how, and a distribution network all over the UK. Unless we do this, and soon, we will lose existing custom to our competitors and will be unable to expand, because we do not have additional storage or distribution capacity.

Note: ® stands for registered trademark (= eingetragenes Markenzeichen).

Comprehension

Task 1

Read the report which was prepared by Michael Carson, the new sales director of the family firm Carson and Sons Ltd, for the board of directors. He wants to persuade the other directors to take an important decision. Answer the following questions.

a. What information is given under "terms of reference"?

b. How many years are considered in the report?

c. Why has there been a change in the sales figures?

d. What are "domestic sales"?

e. Sum up the main problems of distribution for Carson an Sons' products in your own words.

f. What does the writer of the report recommend?

g. The word "outsourcing" is used in German too. Can you explain what it means?

h. Would you have made the same recommendations? Give reasons for your answer.

i. Write a short account in German of the contents of the report.

Activity

Writing reports

Task 2

Match a heading with a definition:

Heading	Definition
Terms of Reference (Aufgabenbereich)	a. The facts you have found out or the information you have collected.
Proceedings (Vorgehensweise)	b. The subject of the report, who it is for, when it was written and who wrote it.
Findings (Untersuchungsergebnisse)	c. How the information in the report was collected.
Conclusion (Schlussfolgerung)	d. Your advice about what should be done.
Recommendation (Empfehlung)	e. The result you come to, on the basis of the facts.

Note: You do not always have to use the headings which are used in the above report, but using them makes the presentation of your information look more professional.
The headings have a German translation, but you would not use the German headings in the same way as the English ones.

Business Tip!

How to write a good report

– Collect your facts. Organise your facts and present them objectively. Your opinion is expressed in your recommendation at the end.

– Use a simple style.

– Do not use emotional language, e. g. write "office work cannot be carried out efficiently", not "the office organisation is a terrible mess".

– Do not use short forms such as "isn't", or "doesn't".

– Link the sections of your report and include a summary of the main points at the end.

Activity

Report writing

Task 3

Find pairs of sentences with approximately the same meaning.

Emotional style	Factual style
That is rubbish.	It may be necessary to take out a loan.
This will bring a terrible slump in profits.	Some company re-organisation is advisable.
There is an immense risk that we will suffer huge losses.	Prices have risen considerably.
The way prices have shot up is unbelievable.	This will lead to a decrease in profits.
We will probably be forced to borrow money from the bank.	I do not agree with you.
The whole company is in a terrible mess; it will be a disaster if we don't change things immediately.	Financial losses cannot be ruled out.

Task 4

What are the long forms of the underlined words in the sentences below?

a. <u>He's</u> not in the office today.
b. <u>She's</u> got a day off.
c. <u>I'd</u> like a glass of water, please.
d. He said <u>he'd</u> already finished.
e. It <u>isn't</u> time to go yet.
f. If <u>I'd</u> the time, <u>I'd</u> go.

Report-writing practice

Task 5

Using the report "Distribution of Carson's Natural Beauty Products® in the UK" as a model, write a short report on one of the following:

- Public transport in your town or village: present situation and recommended policy.
- Activities for young people in your area: present situation and recommended policy.
- Freight transport on European roads: present situation and recommended policy.

Security in the USA

Since the historic 9/11 (11th of September 2001) when the World Trade Centre was destroyed, the USA has tightened up on border security. There are special security requirements for any goods entering the USA. To increase security, the Customs and Border Protection (U.S. Department of Homeland Security) has set up a new system called C-TPAT (Customs-Trade Partnership against Terrorism). For updated information see www.cbp.gov. The following is an extract from the old website www.customs.gov (accessed June 2003):

U.S. Customs and Border Protection

C-TPAT Fact Sheet and Frequently Asked Questions

What is C-TPAT?

- C-TPAT is a joint government-business initiative to build cooperative relationships that strengthen overall supply chain and border security.
- C-TPAT recognises that Customs can provide the highest level of security only through close cooperation with the ultimate owners of the supply chain, importers, carriers, brokers, warehouse operators and manufacturers.
- Through this initiative, Customs is asking businesses to ensure the integrity of their security practices and communicate their security guidelines to their business partners within the supply chain.

What does participation in C-TPAT require?

Businesses must apply to participate in C-TPAT. Participants will sign an agreement that commits them to the following actions:
- Conduct a comprehensive self-assessment of supply chain security using the C-TPAT security guidelines jointly developed by Customs and the trade community. The guidelines encompass the following areas: Procedural Security, Physical Security, Personnel Security, Education and Training, Access Controls, Manifest Procedures, and Conveyance Security.
- Submit a supply chain security profile questionnaire to Customs.
- Develop and implement a program to enhance security throughout the supply chain in accordance with C-TPAT guidelines.
- Communicate C-TPAT guidelines to other companies in the supply chain and work toward building the guidelines into relationships with these companies.

What are the benefits of participation in C-TPAT?

C-TPAT offers businesses an opportunity to play an active role in the war against terrorism. By participating in this first worldwide supply chain security initiative, companies will ensure a more secure supply chain for their employees, suppliers and customers. Beyond these essential security benefits, Customs will offer potential benefits to C-TPAT members including:
- A reduced number of inspections (reduced border times)
- An assigned account manager
- Access to the C-TPAT membership list
- Eligibility for account-based processes (bimonthly/monthly payments, e. g.)
- An emphasis on self-policing, not Customs verification

Comprehension

Task 6

Answer the following questions:

a. What is the main purpose of Customs controls in most countries?
b. Had you heard of the C-TPAT?
c. What is the main aim of C-TPAT?
d. How could it be relevant to European forwarding companies?
e. What could be the disadvantages of exporting goods to a North American company which is not a member of C-TPAT?

Task 7

Match each word to its definition.

An importer …	… arranges customs clearance for his customers (especially in the USA).
Personnel Security …	… has to do with the way the goods in a consignment are listed and checked.
A manufacturer …	… works at a border post, an airport or a port and checks the goods which come into or go out of the country.
A carrier …	… owns or manages a factory which produces goods.
Conveyance Security …	… has to do with how many people can look at the data of the company.
A participant …	… works in a special building in which goods are stored.
A customs officer …	… takes part in a meeting or a project.
A warehouse operator …	… owns or manages a company which transports freight.
Manifest Procedures …	… has to do with employees and where they come from.
A broker …	… ships goods into the country from abroad, in order to sell them.
Access Controls …	… has to do with the vehicles used.

Task 8

Match each word in A with a word from B which means (almost) the same.

A	B
enhance (verb)	make sure of (verb)
participant	improve (verb)
benefit (noun)	advantage
verification	member
ensure (verb)	shared (between two)
joint (adj)	check

Activity

Security in the USA

Task 9

Discuss the following questions with your partner.

a. In what ways can people at airports or ports check that there are no explosives or weapons in luggage or packages?
b. What happened on September 11th 2001?
c. Why did this have an influence on procedures in ports and airports and at borders?

Vocabulary trainer

British and American English

Spelling

British English		American English	
-ae	anaesthetic	-e	anesthetic
-oe	oestrogen	-e	estrogen
-ence	licence	-ense	license
-re	centre	-er	center
-our	labour	-or	labor
-ogue	dialogue	-og	dialog
-ou	mould	-o	mold
-ll	traveller	-l	traveler

(Tip: set the spell-checker on your PC to the variety you want to use.)

Task 10

Below are some common pairs of words which are different in British and American English. Match the pairs.

British English	American English
bill	elevator
car	first floor
plane	check
lift	aircraft
city centre	movie theater

British English	American English
autumn	candy
toilet	trash
banknote	bill
cinema	Maitre d'
rubbish	fall
sweets	billfold
head waiter	round trip (ticket)
ground floor	automobile
petrol	rest room/bathroom
wallet	downtown
return (ticket)	gasoline

Logistics and ecology

"Just-in-Time" deliveries, back in the Eighties, were not popular with people who were worried about ecology. The trouble was that instead of one big delivery, companies wanted a lot of smaller deliveries, which meant more goods vehicles on the roads. However, modern logistics has a number of solutions for this. The main key word is consolidation. Through careful planning and use of data from IT systems, loads can be put together in various ways to avoid driving around with an empty or half-empty lorry.

Consolidation is not a new word. It too has been around at least since the Sixties. It has been used for many years in connection with both container traffic and air freight. Containers, for example, only really make sense if they are full, but not every shipper has enough goods to make up an FCL (Full Container Load). So consolidators or groupage agents put together a number of smaller loads (LCLs: Less than Container Loads) to make up FCLs. This means that the shipper can send the load more cheaply, and the groupage agent organises deconsolidation when the container arrives, that is, he sees to it that each consignment is sent to the right consignee. However, traditionally, much of this consolidation work has been on shipments to destinations overseas, and less for transport inside Europe.

Consolidation is also used by consolidation agents for air freight. Air freight tariffs are proportionally cheaper for bulk loads. A consolidator books bulk space over sectors where there is normally a lot of freight traffic. He gets a quantity discount for this space, and then he puts together a number of smaller consignments from individual shippers and dispatches them on the reserved plane. At the airport of destination, a receiving agent takes care of sending the separate consignments on to the correct consignee.

Logistic service providers can consolidate goods inside any country or across countries, whether they are consumer goods or materials for industrial production lines. They can do this by putting together loads from different customers, and, to make sure that they use maximum capacity, they can store goods short-term at suitable points in the network, carry out cross-docking and so on. This not only helps to satisfy the customers and to reduce costs, it also helps to protect the environment. Fewer trips mean less exhaust fumes and less consumption of energy.

Consolidation is not the only logistics tool. There are many more. But the above example shows that good logistics management is good not only for profits, but also for the environment.

Comprehension

Task 11

a. What is the main ecological disadvantage of "JIT"?
b. Explain in your own words what is meant by "deconsolidation".
c. What is meant by "cross-docking"? (If you do not know, look it up on the internet.)
d. Suggest some other ways to reduce fuel consumption in the logistics industry.

Reference section

Business communications

English spelling

A	eh	for	Andrew
B	bie	for	Benjamin
C	ssie	for	Charlie
D	die	for	David
E	ie	for	Edward
F	eff	for	Freddie
G	djie	for	George
H	ehtsch	for	Harry
I	ei	for	Isabel
J	djeh	for	Jack
K	keh	for	Katie
L	ell	for	Lucy
M	emm	for	Mary
N	enn	for	Nellie
O	oh	for	Oliver
P	pie	for	Peter
Q	kyou	for	Quentin
R	ah	for	Richard
S	ess	for	Susan
T	tie	for	Thomas
U	you	for	Ursula
V	wie	for	Victor
W	dabbelyou	for	William
X	ächs	for	X-ray
Y	why	for	Yvonne
Z	zed	for	Zoë

– dash (minus) · / slash · \ back slash · @ at · . dot · small letters (lower case) · CAPITAL LETTERS (upper case) · italics · bold · ü = u Umlaut oder ue · neues Wort = new word · underscore · underline

Notes for business letters in English

The date

Decide on one form of writing the date, and always use it.
All-figure dates (although often used in international correspondence) can cause confusion because:
- Europeans write day/month/year: 04.05.2014 = 4th May 2014
- Americans and many Asians write month/day/year: 04.05.2014 = April 5th 2014

The address on the envelope

Always copy precisely the address you have been given; if there is a postal code, copy it in full.
When sending a letter to another country, write the name of the town and country of destination in capital letters, and do not use abbreviations (except "USA").

from the UK	from Germany
Ms H Howard 59 Nine Elms Road Wilmslow Cheshire SK9 6AA	Ms H Howard 59 Nine Elms Road Wilmslow Cheshire GREAT BRITAIN SK9 6AA
Mr Bill Brook 1623 Dexter Street WASHINGTON DC 20260-6532 USA	Mr Bill Brook 1623 Dexter Street WASHINGTON DC 20260-6532 USA

The salutation

If you are on first-name terms: Dear John/Dear Mary
If you are not on first-name terms: Dear Mr Jones/Dear Ms Jones
You should write Ms before a woman's family name if you do not know her marital status.
If you do not know a name, write: Dear Sir or Madam/Ladies and Gentlemen
(It is, however, better to find out the name of a contact person in the company if possible.)

The close

The close should fit the salutation.

Salutation	Close	
	British	**American**
Dear John	Yours sincerely Best regards	Kind regards Best regards
Dear Mr Jones	Yours sincerely	Sincerely yours Best regards
Dear Sir	Yours faithfully	Sincerely (yours)
Dear Sirs	Yours faithfully	
Ladies and Gentlemen		Yours truly

If you enclose documents or photos with the letter, write "Enc." in the bottom left corner of the final page of the letter (Enc. = Enclosures = Anlagen).

Some useful expressions for letter-writing

Check that you know the German translation for each expression.
Starting a letter or fax to a new contact:
- Your company was recommended to us by Smith and Sons Ltd.
- We saw your product at the Book Fair in Frankfurt.
- We refer to your advertisement in The Times concerning …
- We are/I am writing to you about …

Starting a reply:
- Thank you for your letter/enquiry/fax/telephone call of 20th June.
- With reference to our telephone call this morning, I would like to confirm that …
- In reply to your letter of 30th September.
- I acknowledge receipt of your letter of 2nd July.

Making a request/enquiry:
- Please send us your current price list.
- We would like to enquire about your new range of electrical goods.
- (Could you) please tell us whether you can deliver within seven days?
- I would be grateful if you would send me a list of stockists in the area.

Answering a request/enquiry:
- Thank you for your letter/enquiry/fax of …
- In answer to your question …
- Please find enclosed …
- Please find attached …
- I am sending … with this fax.

Confirmation:
- I am writing to confirm the order for 200 office chairs (type W34) made by telephone this morning.
- I hereby confirm the following order (your reference number Q/45 79) at the prices quoted in your fax of October 10th.

Complaints:
- The consignment we received from you this morning contained goods which do not conform to the samples you sent us.
- We have just received your delivery of the above order. I regret to inform you that …
- I am writing to complain about …
- When we placed the above-mentioned order five weeks ago we specified a delivery period of three weeks.
- We find this situation unsatisfactory.

Apologies:
- We apologise for the late delivery of …
- We are sorry that the above consignment arrived damaged.
- We apologise for any inconvenience caused.

Closing phrases:
- We/I look forward to hearing from you.
- Thank you in advance for your help.
- If you have any questions please do not hesitate to contact us/me.

Conversion tables for metric and imperial measures

Linear Measure

Imperial	Imperial	Metric
	1 inch (1)	25.4 mm
12 inches = 1 foot	1 foot (1)	304.8 mm
3 feet = 1 yard	1 yard (1 yd)	914.4 mm
1760 yd = 1 mile	1 mile (= statute mile)	1.609
0.0397 inch	0.0397 inch	1 mm
0.3937 inch	0.3937 inch	1 cm
39.37 inches	39.37 inches	1 m
3.281 feet	3.281 feet	1 m

Weight

Imperial (avoirdupois)	Imperial (avoirdupois)	Metric
	1 ounce (1oz)	28.3495 g
16 oz = 1 lb	1 pound (1 lb)	0.4536 kg*
14 lb = 1 st	1 stone (1 st)	
28 lb = 1 qr	1 quarter (qr)	12.7006 kg
4 qr (112 lb) = 1 cwt	1 cwt (hundredweight)	50.8024 kg
20 cwt = 1 UK ton/long ton	1 long ton	1.0605 tonnes**
1 short ton (USA)	1 short ton	0.9072 tonnes

* Ounces: the same word "ounce" is used in two separate measurement systems for weight:
There is also a "Troy ounce": the troy system is used for weithing jewels.
A Troy ounce = 31.1035 g

** Tons and tons:
One tonne (European ton) = 1000 kg. It is a good idea to check whether the tons are tonnes, UK tons or short tons, when dealing with countries outside Europe which have not signed the metric convenion.

Liquid measure
(Note again the differences between UK and US measures.)

Imperial	Metric
1 fluid ounce (fl.oz)	28.413 cm^3 UK
	29.573 cm^3 US
1 pint (pt)	568.261 cm^3 UK
	473.163 cm^3 US
1 quart (qt)	1.136 litres UK
	1.101 litres US
1 gallon (gal)	4.546 litres UK
	3.785 litres US

Incoterms 2013

	Short form	Long form	applicable to
Group E (seller does not pay for carriage)	EXW	Ex works (named place)	any form of transport
Group F (seller does not pay for main carriage)	FCA	Free Carrier (named place)	any form of transport
	FAS	Free Alongside Ship (named port of departure)	shipment by ship only*
	FOB	Free On Board (named port of departure)	shipment by ship only*
Group C (seller pays for main carriage)	CFR	Cost and Freight (named destination port)	shipment by ship only*
	CIF	Cost, Insurance, Freight (named destination port)	shipment by ship only*
	CPT	Carriage paid to (named place of destination)	any form of transport
	CIP	Carriage and Insurance Paid to (named place of destination)	any form of transport
Group D (seller pays for carriage)	DAT**	Delivered at Terminal	any form of transport
	DAP**	Delivered at Place	any form of transport
	DDP	Delivered Duty Paid (named destination)	any form of transport

*   ocean, coastal or inland waterway
** The terms DAT and DAP are new; they replace the terms DAF, DES, DEQ and DDU in the Incoterms 2000 list.

Irregular verbs

infinitive 1. Form	past tense 2. Form	past participle 3. Form	deutsche Bedeutung
be	was, were	been	sein
become	became	become	werden
begin	began	begun	beginnen
break	broke	broken	(zer)brechen
bring	brought	brought	(her)bringen
build	built	built	(er)bauen
buy	bought	bought	kaufen
catch	caught	caught	fangen
choose	chose	chosen	(aus)wählen
come	came	come	kommen
cost	cost	cost	kosten
cut	cut	cut	schneiden
deal	dealt	dealt	handeln
do	did	done	tun, machen
drink	drank	drunk	trinken
drive	drove	driven	fahren
eat	ate	eaten	essen
fall	fell	fallen	fallen
feel	felt	felt	(sich) fühlen
fight	fought	fought	kämpfen
find	found	found	finden
forget	forgot	forgotten	vergessen
get	got	got	bekommen
give	gave	given	geben
go	went	gone	gehen
grow	grew	grown	wachsen, ansteigen
hang	hung	hung	hängen
have	had	had	haben
hear	heard	heard	hören
hold	held	held	halten
keep	kept	kept	behalten

Irregular verbs

infinitive 1. Form	past tense 2. Form	past participle 3. Form	deutsche Bedeutung
know	knew	known	wissen
lead	led	led	führen
leave	left	left	verlassen
lend	lent	lent	(ver)leihen
let	let	let	(zu)lassen
lose	lost	lost	verlieren
make	made	made	machen, tun
mean	meant	meant	bedeuten
meet	met	met	treffen
pay	paid	paid	zahlen
put	put	put	setzen, stellen, legen
read	read	read	lesen
ride	rode	ridden	fahren, reiten
ring	rang	rung	anrufen, läuten
rise	rose	risen	(an)steigen
run	ran	run	laufen, betreiben
say	said	said	sagen
see	saw	seen	sehen
sell	sold	sold	verkaufen
send	sent	sent	schicken
show	showed	shown	zeigen
shut	shut	shut	schließen
sing	sang	sung	singen
sit	sat	sat	sitzen
sleep	slept	slept	schlafen
speak	spoke	spoken	sprechen
spend	spent	spent	verbringen, ausgeben
stand	stood	stood	stehen
steal	stole	stolen	stehlen
swim	swam	swum	schwimmen
take	took	taken	nehmen, dauern
teach	taught	taught	lehren
tell	told	told	erzählen
think	thought	thought	glauben, denken
throw	threw	thrown	werfen
understand	understood	understood	verstehen
wake	woke	woken	(er)wachen
wear	wore	worn	(Kleidung) tragen
win	won	won	gewinnen
write	wrote	written	schreiben

Vocabulary (unit-based)

UNIT 1

old-fashioned	[ˌəʊldˈfæʃənd]	altmodisch
view	[vjuː]	Meinung
freight forwarder	[ˈfreɪt ˌfɔːwədə]	Spediteur
heavy-weight	[ˈheviweɪt]	Schwergewicht
trucker	[ˈtrʌkə]	Lastwagenfahrer
century	[ˈsentʃəri]	Jahrhundert
trade	[treɪd]	Handel
trader	[ˈtreɪdə]	Händler
selection	[sɪˈlekʃən]	Auswahl
goods	[gʊdz]	Güter / Waren
imagine (v)	[ɪˈmædʒɪn]	sich vorstellen
manufacturer	[ˌmænjəˈfæktʃərə]	Hersteller
manufacture (v)	[ˌmænjəˈfæktʃə]	herstellen
sell (v)	[sel]	verkaufen
sales	[seɪlz]	Verkäufe
responsible for	[rɪˈspɒnsəbl ˌfɔː]	verantwortlich für
in good condition	[ɪn gʊd kənˈdɪʃən]	in gutem Zustand
supply chain	[səˈplaɪ ˌtʃeɪn]	Versorgungskette
consumer	[kənˈsjuːmə]	Verbraucher(in)
available	[əˈveɪləbl]	verfügbar
household goods	[ˈhaʊshəʊld ˌgʊdz]	Haushaltsgüte
equipment	[ɪˈkwɪpmənt]	Ausstattung / Bedarf
stock	[stɒk]	Lagebestand
raw material	[ˌrɔː məˈtɪəriəl]	Rohstoff
finished product	[ˈfɪnɪʃt ˈprɒdʌkt]	Fertigprodukt
movement	[ˈmuːvmənt]	Bewegung
loss	[lɒs]	Verlust
offer (v)	[ˈɒfə]	anbieten
offer	[ˈɒfə]	Angebot
provide (v)	[prəˈvaɪd]	anbieten / zur Verfügung stellen
warehouse	[ˈweəhaʊs]	Lager
warehousing	[ˈweəhaʊzɪŋ]	Lagerung
warehouse (v)	[ˈweəhaʊz]	lagern
organise (v)	[ˈɔːgənaɪz]	organisieren
tracing and tracking	[ˈtreɪsɪŋ ænd ˈtrækɪŋ]	Sendungsverfolgung
world	[wɜːld]	Welt
spend (v) time	[ˌspend ˈtaɪm]	Zeit verbringen
opportunity	[ˌɒpəˈtjuːnəti]	Gelegenheit
description	[dɪˈskrɪpʃən]	Beschreibung
function (v)	[ˈfʌŋkʃən]	funktionieren
co-operate (v)	[kəʊˈɒpəreɪt]	kooperieren
produce (v)	[prəˈdjuːs]	herstellen / produzieren
distribution (department)	[ˌdɪstrɪˈbjuːʃən (dɪˈpɑːtmənt)]	Vertrieb(sabteilung)
part	[pɑːt]	Teil

supply (v)	[sə'plaɪ]	liefern / beliefern
on demand	[ˌɒn dɪ'mɑːnd]	auf Abruf
main task	['meɪn ˌtɑːsk]	Hauptaufgabe
deal with (v)	['diːl ˌwɪð]	sich kümmern um
delivery	[dɪ'lɪvəri]	Lieferung
customer	['kʌstəmə]	Kunde
order	['ɔːdə]	Bestellung
order (v)	['ɔːdə]	bestellen
airfreight	['eəfreɪt]	Luftfracht
check (v)	[tʃek]	überprüfen
schedule	['ʃedjuːl, 'ʃedʒuːl, 'skedjuːl, 'skedʒuːl]	Zeitplan
book (v)	[bʊk]	buchen / reservieren
prepare (v)	[prɪ'pɜə]	vorbereiten
necessary	['nesəsəri]	notwendig
document	['dɒkjəmənt]	Papier / Dokument
decision	[dɪ'sɪʒən]	Entscheidung
decide (v)	[dɪ'saɪd]	entscheiden
calculate (v)	['kælkjəleɪt]	kalkulieren
job	[dʒɒb]	Aufgabe/ Arbeitsstelle
assembly line	[ə'sembli ˌlaɪn]	Montageband
automotive company	[ˌɔːtə'məʊtɪv ˌkʌmpəni]	Autohersteller
lose (v)	[luːz]	verlieren
contract	['kɒntrækt]	Vertrag
describe (v)	[dɪ'skraɪb]	beschreiben
solve (v)	[sɒlv]	lösen
boring	['bɔːrɪŋ]	langweilig
do sport (v)	[ˌdu 'spɔːt]	Sport machen
gym	[dʒɪm]	Fitnesscenter / Turnhalle
security	[sɪ'kjʊərəti]	Sicherheit
regulation	[ˌregjə'leɪʃən]	Vorschrift
rule	[ruːl]	Regel
shipment	['ʃɪpmənt]	Warensendung / Sendung
luckily	['lʌkɪli]	glücklicherweise
handle (v) (freight)	['hændl (freɪt)]	umschlagen (Fracht)
fork-lift truck	[ˌfɔːklɪft 'trʌk]	Gabelstapler
truck driver/ heavy goods vehicle driver/ lorry driver	['trʌk ˌdraɪvə / ˌhevi 'gʊdz ˌvɪəkl ˌdraɪvə / 'lɒri ˌdraɪvə]	Lastwagenfahrer
gantry crane	['gæntrɪ ˌkreɪn]	Portalkran
delivery van	[dɪ'lɪvəri ˌvæn]	Lieferwagen
heavy goods vehicle / lorry / truck	[ˌhevi 'gʊdz ˌvɪəkl / 'lɒri / trʌk]	Lastwagen
experienced	[ɪk'spɪəriənst]	erfahren
wanted	['wɒntɪd]	gesucht
be able to (v)	[bɪ 'eɪbl tu]	können
require (v)	[rɪ'kwaɪə]	benötigen
applicant	['æplɪkənt]	Bewerber(in)
cool-chain	['kuːltʃeɪn]	Kühlkette
supervise (v)	['suːpəvaɪz]	beaufsichtigen

gas station (US), petrol station (GB)	['gæs ˌsteɪʃən], ['petrəl ˌsteɪʃən]	Tankstelle
load (v)	[ləʊd]	laden
found (v)	[faʊnd]	begründen / gründen
dock worker	['dɒk ˌwɜːkə]	Hafenarbeiter
lift (v)	[lɪft]	heben
trailer	['treɪlə]	Anhänger
earn (v)	[ɜːn]	verdienen
on board	[ˌɒn 'bɔːd]	an Bord
develop (v)	[dɪ'veləp]	entwickeln
box	[bɒks]	Kiste
mode of transport	[məʊd ɒf 'trænspɔːt]	Transportmittel
rail	[reɪl]	Bahn
successful	[sək'sesfʊl]	erfolgreich
cargo	['kɑːgəʊ]	Fracht
container-ship	[kən'teɪnə ʃɪp]	Containerschiff
port	[pɔːt]	Hafen
channel	['tʃænəl]	Kanal
access	['ækses]	Zugang
expand (v)	[ɪk'spænd]	expandieren
quay	[kiː]	Kai
take over (v)	[ˌteɪk 'əʊvə]	übernehmen
sailing ship	['seɪlɪŋ ʃɪp]	Segelschiff
speed	[spiːd]	Geschwindigkeit
insurance	[ɪn'ʃʊərəns]	Versicherung

UNIT 2

distributing company	[dɪ'strɪbjuːtɪŋ 'kʌmpəni]	Vertriebsgesellschaft
abroad	[ə'brɔːd]	Ausland
strawberry	['strɔːbəri]	Erdbeere
oil	[ɔɪl]	Öl
standstill	['stændstɪl]	Stillstand
maintain (v)	[meɪn'teɪn]	erhalten
balance of trade	[ˌbæləns ɒf 'treɪd]	Handelsbilanz
reputation	[ˌrepjə'teɪʃən]	Ruf
reliable	[rɪ'laɪəbl]	zuverlässig
customs	['kʌstəmz]	Zoll
forbidden	[fə'bɪdən]	verboten
restrict (v)	[rɪ'strɪkt]	begrenzen
weapon	['wepən]	Waffe
authority	[ɔː'θɒrəti]	Behörde
smuggle (v)	['smʌgl]	schmuggeln
health	[helθ]	Gesundheit
comply with (v)	[kəm'plaɪ ˌwɪð]	einhalten
protect (v)	[prəʊ'tekt]	schützen
disease	[dɪ'ziːz]	Krankheit
duty (customs duty)	['djuːti ('kʌstəmz ˌdjuːti)]	Zollabgabe
member	['membə]	Mitglied
declare (v)	[dɪ'kleə]	deklarieren

value	['væljuː]	Wert
clear (v) (through customs)	[klɪə (θruː 'kʌstəmz)]	abfertigen
dutiable	['djuːtiəbl], ['dʒuː-]	zu verzollen
bonded store	[ˌbɒndɪd 'stɔː]	Zolllager
create (v)	[kri'eɪt]	erzeugen
revenue	['revənjuː]	Einkommen
domestic	[də'mestɪk]	einheimisch
quota	['kwəʊtə]	Kontingent
tariff	['tærɪf]	Tarif
classify (v)	['klæsɪfaɪ]	klassifizieren
commodity	[kə'mɒdəti]	Ware
digit	['dɪdʒɪt]	Zahl
sample	['sɑːmpl]	Muster
appointment	[ə'pɔɪntmənt]	Termin
connect (v)	[kə'nekt]	verbinden
mobile phone (GB)	[ˌməʊbaɪl 'fəʊn]	Handy
cell phone (USA)	['sel ˌfəʊn]	Handy
message	['mesɪdʒ]	Nachricht
(telephone) line	[('telɪfəʊn) laɪn]	Leitung
caller	['kɔːlə]	Anrufer
promise	['prɒmɪs]	Versprechen
instructions	[ɪn'strʌkʃənz]	Anleitung
role	[rəʊl]	Rolle
caller	['kɔːlə]	Anrufer
repeat (v)	[rɪ'piːt]	wiederholen
say goodbye (v)	[ˌseɪ ɡʊd'baɪ]	sich verabschieden
pass on (a message) (v)	[ˌpɑːs 'ɒn (ə 'mesɪdʒ)]	weiterleiten
introduce (yourself) (v)	['ɪntrədjuːs (jɔː'self)]	sich melden
polite / politely	[pə'laɪt], [pə'laɪtli]	höflich
confirm (v)	[kən'fɜːm]	bestätigen
component	[kəm'pəʊnənt]	Komponente
apologise (v)	[ə'pɒlədʒaɪz]	sich entschuldigen
promise (v)	['prɒmɪs]	versprechen
out of order	[ˌaʊt ɒf 'ɔːdə]	außer Betrieb
practise (v)	['præktɪs]	üben
complaint	[kəm'pleɪnt]	Beschwerde
pour (v)	[pɔː]	gießen
be lucky (v)	[bɪ 'lʌki]	Glück haben
favour	['feɪvə]	Bitte
mean (v)	[miːn]	bedeuten / sagen wollen
go on (v)	[ˌɡəʊ 'ɒn]	weiter machen / weiter sprechen
wonder (v)	['wʌndə]	sich fragen
if it's not too much trouble	[ɪf ɪts nɒt tuː mʌtʃ 'trʌbl]	wenn es Ihnen nicht zu viel ausmacht
ride (v) (a motorbike)	[raɪd (ə 'məʊtəbaɪk)]	Motorrad fahren
That sounds fantastic.	[ðæt saʊndz fæn'tæstɪk]	Das hört sich fantastisch an.
dream	[driːm]	Traum
true	[truː]	wahr

specialise (v)	['speʃəlaɪz]	spezialisieren
ship (v)	[ʃɪp]	transportieren / verschiffen
customised	['kʌstəmaɪzd]	auf Kundenwunsch gefertigt
valuable	['væljuəbl]	wertvoll
safe(ly)	['seɪf(li)]	sicher
risk	[rɪsk]	Risiko
worry (v)	['wʌri]	sich Sorgen machen
damage (v)	['dæmɪdʒ]	beschädigen
Would you mind …?	[ˌwʊd ju 'maɪnd]	Hätten Sie was dagegen …?
head of department	[ˌhed ɒf dɪ'pɑːtmənt]	Abteilungsleiter (-in)
hang up (v) (on phone)	[ˌhæŋ 'ʌp (ɒn fəʊn)]	auflegen / ein Telefonat beenden
purchasing (department)	['pɜːtʃəsɪŋ (dɪ'pɑːtmənt)]	Einkauf(sabteilung)
chain	[tʃeɪn]	Kette
headquarters	['hedkwɔːtəz]	Hauptquartier / Hauptsitz
unfortunately	[ʌn'fɔːtʃnətli]	leider
consignment	[kən'saɪnmənt]	Sendung
several	['sevərəl]	mehrere
complain (v)	[kəm'pleɪn]	sich beschweren
in demand	[ˌɪn dɪ'mɑːnd]	gefragt
store	[stɔː]	Geschäft
custom	['kʌstəm]	Kundschaft
supplier	[sə'plaɪə]	Zulieferer
dialling code	['daɪəlɪŋ ˌkəʊd]	Vorwahl
press (v)	[pres]	drucken
office hours	['ɒfɪs ˌaʊəz]	Arbeitsstunden
Bother!	['bɒðə]	Verflixt!
I'll put you on hold.	[aɪl 'pʊt ju ɒn 'həʊld]	Ich setze Sie in die Warteschlange.
order number	['ɔːdə ˌnʌmbə]	Bestellungsnummer
Hang on a minute!	[hæŋ 'ɒn ə ˌmɪnɪt]	Warten Sie einen Moment!
slash	[slæʃ]	Schrägstrich
transfer (a call)	[trænsˈfɜːr (ə kɔːl)]	durchstellen
advertise (v)	['ædvətaɪz]	Werbung machen für
dispatch (v)	[dɪ'spætʃ]	versenden
happen (v)	['hæpən]	passieren
extension number	[ɪk'stenʃən ˌnʌmbə]	Durchwahl
Please note!	[ˌpliːz 'nəʊt]	Bitte merken!
change (v)	[tʃeɪndʒ]	ändern
attached file	[əˌtætʃt 'faɪl]	Anhang
according to	[ə'kɔːdɪŋ tu]	gemäß
pallet	['pælɪt]	Palette
footwear	['fʊtweə]	Schuhe
accept (v)	[ək'sept]	akzeptieren
responsibility	[rɪˌspɒnsə'bɪləti]	Verantwortung
in addition	[ˌɪn ə'dɪʃən]	zusätzlich
copy	['kɒpi]	Kopie
commercial invoice	[kə'mɜːʃəl 'ɪnvɔɪs]	Handelsrechnung
ASAP = as soon as possible	[eɪ es eɪ piː], [æz suːn æz 'pɒsəbl]	so bald wie möglich

subject line	['sʌbdʒɪkt ˌlaɪn]	Bezugszeile
customs officer	['kʌstəmz ˌɒfɪsə]	Zollbeamter
per day	[ˌpɜː 'deɪ]	pro Tag
No. (number)	['nʌmbə]	Anzahl
quantity	['kwɒntəti]	Menge
article number	['ɑːtɪkl ˌnʌmbə]	Artikelnummer
price	[praɪs]	Preis
VAT (value added tax)	[viː eɪ tiː ('væljuː 'ædɪd tæks)]	MwSt (Mehrwertsteuer)
final total	['faɪnəl 'təʊtəl]	Endsumme
telephone receiver	['telɪfəʊn rɪ'siːvə]	Telefonhörer
asterisk	['æstərɪsk]	Sternchen

UNIT 3

surface transport	['sɜːfəs 'trænspɔːt]	Land- und Seetransport
advise (v)	[əd'vaɪz]	beraten
depend on (v)	[dɪ'pend ˌɒn]	abhängen von
weight	[weɪt]	Gewicht
size	[saɪz]	Größe
destination	[destɪ'neɪʃən]	Bestimmungsort
reckon (v)	['rekən]	kalkulieren
altogether	[ˌɔːltə'geðə]	insgesamt
approximately	[ə'prɒksɪmətli]	circa / zirka
perishable	['perɪʃəbl]	verderblich
grain	[greɪn]	Korn
tailor-made	['teɪləmeɪd]	maßgeschnitten
quote / quotation	[kwəʊt], [kwəʊ'teɪʃən]	Preisvorschlag / Angebot
ferry	['feri]	Fähre
main road	['meɪn ˌrəʊd]	Hauptstraße
semi-trailer / articulated lorry	['semiˌtreɪlə / ɑːˌtɪkjəleɪtɪd 'lɒri]	Sattelaufliege
roadworthiness	['rəʊdˌwɜːðɪnəs]	Verkehrstauglichkeit
load	[ləʊd]	Ladung
secure (v)	[sɪ'kjʊə]	sichern
break	[breɪk]	Pause
fine	[faɪn]	Bußgeld
increase (v)	[ɪn'kriːs]	zunehmen / steigern
fuel	['fjuːəl]	Brennstoff
toll	[təʊl]	Maut
motorway / highway	['məʊtəweɪ / 'haɪweɪ]	Autobahn
maintenance	['meɪntənəns]	Instandhaltung
inevitable	[ɪ'nevɪtəbl]	unvermeidlich
rail track	['reɪl ˌtræk]	Eisenbahngleis
gauge	[geɪdʒ]	Spurbreite
economic	[iːkə'nɒmɪk]	wirtschaftlich
hopper car	['hɒpə ˌkɑː]	Klappdeckelwagen
double-stack car	['dʌblstæk ˌkɑː]	Doppelstock-Containerwagen
goods train	['gʊdz ˌtreɪn]	Güterzug
savings	['seɪvɪŋz]	Ersparnisse
pick-up services	['pɪkʌp ˌsɜːvɪsɪz]	Abholdienste

consist of (v)	[kən'sıst ɒf]	bestehen aus
dry	[draı]	trocken
bulk cargo	['bʌlk ˌkɑːgəʊ]	Massengut
coal	[kəʊl]	Kohle
iron ore	[ˈaıən ˌɔː]	Eisenerz
cement	[sıˈment]	Zement
loose	[luːs]	unverpackt
inland waterways	[ˈınlænd ˈwɔːtəweız]	Binnengewässer
canal	[kəˈnæl]	Kanal
barge	[bɑːdʒ]	Kahn
change	[tʃeındʒ]	Änderung
local	[ˈləʊkəl]	örtlich
expand (v)	[ıkˈspænd]	sich vergrößern
expectation	[ˌekspekˈteıʃən]	Erwartung
vehicle fleet	[ˈvıəkl ˌfliːt]	Fuhrpark
mainland	[ˈmeınlænd]	Festland
on the contrary	[ɒn ðə ˈkɒntrəri]	im Gegenteil
development	[dıˈveləpmənt]	Entwicklung
enquiry	[ınˈkwaıəri]	Anfrage
distance	[ˈdıstəns]	Entfernung
allocate (v)	[ˈæləkeıt]	zuteilen
vehicle	[ˈvıəkl]	Fahrzeug
loading aid	[ˈləʊdıŋ ˌeıd]	Lademittel
road waybill	[ˈrəʊd ˌweıbıl]	Frachtbrief
manifest / cargo list	[ˈmænıfest / ˈkɑːgəʊ ˌlıst]	Ladeliste
in transit	[ˌın ˈtrænsıt]	auf der Durchreise
barcode	[ˈbɑːkəʊd]	Strichcode
invoice	[ˈınvɔıs]	Rechnung
request (v)	[rıˈkwest]	bitten / erbitten
attached	[əˈtætʃt]	im Anhang
receive (v)	[rıˈsiːv]	empfangen
file	[faıl]	Datei
reply (v)	[rıˈplaı]	antworten
compressed	[kəmˈprest]	komprimiert
urgent	[ˈɜːdʒənt]	dringend
suggestion	[səˈdʒestʃən]	Vorschlag
tachograph	[ˈtækəʊgrɑːf]	Tachograph / Fahrtenschreiber
record (v)	[rıˈkɔːd]	aufschreiben / aufnehmen
tamper with (v)	[ˈtæmpə ˌwıð]	fälschen
allowed	[əˈlaʊd]	erlaubt
regulate (v)	[ˈregjəleıt]	regulieren
law	[lɔː]	Gesetz
log (v)	[lɒg]	protokollieren
congestion zone	[kənˈdʒestʃən ˌzəʊn]	Stauzone
polluted	[pəˈluːtıd]	verschmutzt
sticker	[ˈstıkə]	Aufkleber
particle emission	[ˈpɑːtıkl ıˈmıʃən]	Partikelemission / Teilchenemission

amount	[ə'maʊnt]	Menge
exhaust gas	[ɪg'zɔːst ˌgæs]	Abgase
emit (v)	[ɪ'mɪt]	ausstoßen

UNIT 4

tramp ship	['træmp ʃɪp]	Trampschiff
compete (v)	[kəm'piːt]	konkurrieren
Conference lines	['kɒnfərəns ˌlaɪnz]	Konferenzlinien
route	[ruːt]	Route
unitised cargo	['juːnɪtaɪzd 'kɑːgəʊ]	Einheitsladung
stick to (v)	['stɪk ˌtu]	sich halten an
agreement	[ə'griːmənt]	Abmachung
conventional cargo	[kən'ventʃənəl 'kɑːgəʊ]	konventionelle Ladung
invoice (v)	['ɪnvɔɪs]	berechnen
reefer	['riːfə]	Kühlcontainer
plug in (v)	[ˌplʌg 'ɪn]	einstecken
dangerous	['deɪndʒərəs]	gefährlich
stack (v)	[stæk]	stapeln
charge (v)	[tʃɑːdʒ]	berechnen
unload (v)	[ʌn'ləʊd]	löschen / abladen
included	[ɪn'kluːdɪd]	einbeschlossen
cargo handling dues	['kɑːgəʊ 'hændlɪŋ ˌdjuːz]	Umschlagsgebühren
storage	['stɔːrɪdʒ]	Lagerung
requirements	[rɪ'kwaɪəmənts]	Anforderungen
operating costs	['ɒpəreɪtɪŋ ˌkɒsts]	Betriebskosten
surcharge	['sɜːtʃɑːdʒ]	Zuzahlung
currency	['kʌrənsi]	Währung
delay	[dɪ'leɪ]	Verspätung
foreseeable	[fɔː'siːəbl]	vorhersehbar
arrival	[ə'raɪvəl]	Ankunft
departure	[dɪ'pɑːtʃə]	Abfahrt / Abflug
lighter	['laɪtə]	leichter
slot	[slɒt]	Platz
hold	[həʊld]	Frachtraum
deck	[dek]	Deck
wheel	[wiːl]	Rad
stern	[stɜːn]	Heck
ramp	[ræmp]	Rampe
berth	[bɜːθ]	Anlegeplatz
launch (v)	[lɔːntʃ]	einführen
crude oil	['kruːd ˌɔɪl]	Rohöl
cruise ship	['kruːz ʃɪp]	Kreuzfahrtschiff
passenger	['pæsəndʒə]	Passagier
rate	[reɪt]	Preis / Tarif
scheduled	['ʃedjuːld], ['ʃedʒuːld], ['skedjuːld], ['skedʒuːld]	geplant
avoid (v)	[ə'vɔɪd]	vermeiden
short cut	['ʃɔːt ˌkʌt]	Abkürzung
draught (of a ship)	[drɑːft (ɒf ə ʃɪp)]	Tiefgang

handling	['hændlɪŋ]	Umschlag
staff	[stɑːf]	Personal
feeder service	['fiːdə ˌsɜːvɪs]	Zubringerdienst
mark (v)	[mɑːk]	markieren / kennzeichnen
mark	[mɑːk]	Markierung
adhesive	[əd'hiːsɪv]	haftend / Haft-
label	['leɪbəl]	Etikett
instructions	[ɪn'strʌkʃənz]	Anweisungen
fragile	['frædʒaɪl]	zerbrechlich
letter of credit (L/C)	['letər ɒf 'kredɪt], [el siː]	Akkreditiv
otherwise	['ʌðəwaɪz]	sonst
refuse (v)	[rɪ'fjuːz]	verweigern
bill of lading (B/L)	[ˌbɪl ɒf 'leɪdɪŋ], [biː el]	Konnossement / Frachtbrief
certificate of origin	[sə'tɪfɪkət ɒf 'ɒrɪdʒɪn]	Ursprungszeugnis
interface (v)	['ɪntəfeɪs]	Schnittstelle / Interface
transaction	[træn'zækʃən]	Transaktion
release	[rɪ'liːs]	Freigabe
transhipment	[trænz'ʃɪpmənt]	Umladung
inventory	['ɪnvəntri], [ɪn'ventəri]	Inventar
hazardous	['hæzədəs]	gefährlich
binding	['baɪndɪŋ]	verbindlich
on receipt of	[ˌɒn rɪ'siːt ɒf]	beim Empfang
state (v)	[steɪt]	angeben
explosive	[ɪk'spləʊsɪv]	Sprengstoff / explosiv
flammable	['flæməbl]	feuergefährlich
oxidiser	['ɒksɪdaɪzə]	oxidierende Substanz
toxic	['tɒksɪk]	giftig / Gift-
corrosive	[kə'rəʊsɪv]	korrosiv
miscellaneous	[ˌmɪsə'leɪniəs]	sonstig
bleach	[bliːtʃ]	Bleichmittel
toilet cleaner	['tɔɪlət ˌkliːnə]	WC-Reiniger
weed killer	['wiːd ˌkɪlə]	Unkrautvertilgungsmittel

UNIT 5

packing case	['pækɪŋ ˌkeɪs]	Kiste
furniture	['fɜːnɪtʃə]	Möbeln
store / shop	[stɔː], [ʃɒp]	Geschäft
exhibit (v)	[ɪg'zɪbɪt]	ausstellen
firm	[fɜːm]	fest
vague	[veɪg]	vage
costs	[kɒsts]	Kosten
probably	['prɒbəbli]	wahrscheinlich
It would be worthwhile.	[ɪt wʊd bi 'wɜːθwaɪl]	Es würde sich lohnen.
instead of	[ɪn'sted ɒf]	anstatt
consolidation agent	[kənˌsɒlɪ'deɪʃən ˌeɪdʒənt]	Sammelgutspediteur
groupage container	['gruːpɪdʒ kənˌteɪnə]	Sammelcontainer
check (v)	[tʃek]	nachprüfen
approximate	[ə'prɒksɪmət]	ungefähr
insurance premium	[ɪn'ʃʊərəns ˌpriːmiəm]	Versicherungsprämie

packer	['pækə]	Verpacker(in)
stuff (v) (a container)	[stʌf (ə kən'teɪnə)]	packen
tropical climate	['trɒpɪkəl ˌklaɪmət]	tropisches Klima
heat	[hi:t]	Hitze
damp	[dæmp]	Feuchtigkeit
excited	[ɪk'saɪtɪd]	aufgeregt
seal (v)	[si:l]	versiegeln
manually	['mænjuəli]	manuell
fewer	['fju:ə]	weniger
secure	[sɪ'kjʊə]	sicher
registered	['redʒɪstəd]	eingetragen
annually	['ænjuəli]	jährlich
crew	[kru:]	Mannschaft
employee	[ɪm'plɔɪi:], [ˌemplɔɪ'i:]	Arbeitnehmer(in)
break-bulk	['breɪkbʌlk]	Stückgut
separate (v)	['sepəreɪt]	teilen
maritime transport	['mærɪtaɪm 'trænspɔ:t]	Seetransport
standard	['stændəd]	Norm
purpose-built	[ˌpɜ:pəs 'bɪlt]	für einen speziellen Zweck gebaut
cell	[sel]	Zelle
hanging rail	['hæŋɪŋ ˌreɪl]	Kleiderbügelhalter
garment	['gɑ:mənt]	Kleidungsstück
insulate (v)	['ɪnsjəleɪt]	isolieren
steady	['stedi]	stetig / unverändert
insulate	['ɪnsjəleɪt]	isoliert
ventilated	['ventɪleɪtɪd]	ventiliert
hopper	['hɒpə]	Klappdeck
perishable	['perɪʃəbl]	verderblich
wide	[waɪd]	breit
width	[wɪdθ]	Breite
deep	[di:p]	tief
depth	[depθ]	Tiefe
long	[lɒŋ]	lang
length	[leŋθ]	Länge
broad	[brɔ:d]	breit
breadth	[bredθ]	Breite
thick	[θɪk]	dick
thickness	['θɪknəs]	Dicke
high	[haɪ]	hoch
height	[haɪt]	Höhe
weigh (v)	[weɪ]	wiegen
stormy	['stɔ:mi]	stürmisch
accidentally	[ˌæksɪ'dentəli]	ohne Absicht
on purpose	[ɒn 'pɜ:pəs]	absichtlich
prevent (v)	[prɪ'vent]	vermeiden
damage	['dæmɪdʒ]	Schaden
raft	[rɑ:ft]	Floß
rubbish	['rʌbɪʃ]	Abfall

flotsam	['flɒtsəm]	Strandgut
chart (v)	[tʃɑːt]	kartographisch erfassen
researcher	[rɪ'sɜːtʃə]	Forscher
ocean currents	['əʊʃən ˌkʌrənts]	Meeresströmungen
arouse (v)	[ə'raʊz]	erwecken
rubber duck	['rʌbə ˌdʌk]	Badespielzeug / Gummiente
durable	['djʊərəbl]	unverwüstlich
float (v)	[fləʊt]	schwimmen
manage to do something	['mænɪdʒ tu 'duː ˌsʌmθɪŋ]	etwas schaffen
survive (v)	[sə'vaɪv]	überleben
flock	[flɒk]	Schwarm
purpose	['pɜːpəs]	Zweck
sink (v)	[sɪŋk]	sinken
bleach (v)	[bliːtʃ]	bleichen
re.	[riː]	bezüglich / betreffs
procurement	[prə'kjʊəmənt]	Beschaffung / Anschaffung
gasket	['gæskɪt]	Dichtung
confirmation	[ˌkɒnfə'meɪʃən]	Bestätigung
availability	[əˌveɪlə'bɪləti]	Verfügbarkeit
backlog	['bæklɒg]	Auftragsrückstand
back order	[ˌbæk 'ɔːdə]	nicht gelieferte Bestellung
complain (v)	[kəm'pleɪn]	reklamieren
explanation	[ˌekspləˈneɪʃən]	Erklärung
unsatisfactory	[ʌnˌsætɪs'fæktəri]	nicht zufriedenstellend

UNIT 6

air waybill	['eə ˌweɪbɪl]	Luftfrachtbrief
receipt	[rɪ'siːt]	Quittung
proof	[pruːf]	Beweis
co-operation	[kəʊˌɒpə'reɪʃən]	Zusammenarbeit
issue (v) (a document)	['ɪʃuː (ə 'dɒkjəmənt)]	ausstellen
remove (v)	[rɪ'muːv]	entfernen / beheben
print (v)	[prɪnt]	drucken
archive (v)	['ɑːkaɪv]	archivieren
confidentiality	[ˌkɒnfɪdenʃi'æləti]	Vertraulichkeit
target /objective	['tɑːgɪt], [əb'dʒektɪv]	Ziel
carpet	['kɑːpɪt]	Teppich
cut flowers	[ˌkʌt 'flaʊəz]	Schnittblumen
joke	[dʒəʊk]	Witz
processing facility	['prəʊsesɪŋ fə'sɪləti]	Aufbereitungsanlage
area	['eəriə]	Fläche
retail shops	['riːteɪl ʃɒps]	Einzelhandel
meat products	['miːt ˌprɒdʌkts]	Fleischprodukte
vegetables	['vedʒətəblz]	Gemüse
reject (v)	[rɪ'dʒekt]	ablehnen, zurückweisen
agricultural product	[ˌægrɪ'kʌltʃərəl ˌprɒdʌkts]	landwirtschaftliche Produkte
designate (v)	['dezɪgneɪt]	designieren
vet (veterinarian)	[vet (ˌvetərɪ'neəriən)]	Tierarzt

inspector	[ɪnˈspektə]	Inspektor
inspection authority	[ɪnˈspekʃən ɔːˈθɒrəti]	Prüfstelle
acceptable	[əkˈseptəbl]	annehmbar
waste (v)	[weɪst]	verschwenden
ensure (v)	[ɪnˈʃɔː], [-ˈʃʊə]	versichern
hygiene	[ˈhaɪdʒiːn]	Hygiene
overalls	[ˈəʊvərɔːlz]	Arbeitskleidung
hair-net	[ˈheənet]	Haarnetz
cool (v)	[kuːl]	kühlen
ice	[aɪs]	Eis
chemistry	[ˈkemɪstri]	Chemie
diversify (v)	[daɪˈvɜːsɪfaɪ]	diversifizieren
decade	[ˈdekeɪd]	Jahrzehnt
pharmaceutical products	[ˌfɑːməˈsjuːtɪkəl ˌprɒdʌkts]	Arzneimittel
salmon	[ˈsæmən]	Lachs
button	[ˈbʌtən]	Knopf
shape	[ʃeɪp]	Form
dictated	[dɪkˈteɪtɪd]	diktiert / entschieden
danger	[ˈdeɪndʒə]	Gefahr
gap	[gæp]	Lücke
contents	[ˈkɒntents]	Inhalt
endanger (v)	[ɪnˈdeɪndʒə]	gefährden
board	[bɔːd]	Brett
internship / work placement	[ˈɪntɜːnʃɪp], [ˈwɜːk ˌpleɪsmənt]	Praktikum
vacation	[vəˈkeɪʃən]	Semesterferien
opposite	[ˈɒpəzɪt]	Gegenteil
catchment area	[ˈkætʃmənt ˌeəriə]	Einzugsgebiet
connected	[kəˈnektɪd]	verbunden
divided	[dɪˈvaɪdɪd]	geteilt
distribution	[ˌdɪstrɪˈbjuːʃən]	Vertrieb
office accommodation	[ˈɒfɪs əˌkɒməˈdeɪʃən]	Büroräume
facilities	[fəˈsɪlətiz]	Anlagen
live animals	[ˌlaɪv ˈænɪməlz]	lebende Tiere
hazardous goods	[ˈhæzədəs ˌgʊdz]	Gefahrgut
configure (v)	[kənˈfɪgə]	konfigurieren
landing gear	[ˈlændɪŋ ˌgɪə]	Fahrgestell
space shuttle	[ˈspeɪs ˌʃʌtl]	Raumfähre
lock (v)	[lɒk]	verriegeln / verschließen
strap (v)	[stræp]	festbinden
stow (v)	[stəʊ]	stauen
centre of gravity	[ˈsentər ɒf ˈgrævəti]	Schwerpunkt
shift (v)	[ʃɪft]	sich bewegen

UNIT 7

issue (v)	[ˈɪʃuː]	ausstellen
represent (v)	[ˌreprɪˈzent]	vertreten
unite (v)	[juːˈnaɪt]	vereinigen
promote (v)	[prəˈməʊt]	befördern / fördern
uniform	[ˈjuːnɪfɔːm]	einheitlich

vocational training	[vəˈkeɪʃənəl ˈtreɪnɪŋ]	Berufsausbildung
electronic data interchange EDI	[ˌelekˈtrɒnɪk ˈdeɪtə ˈɪntətʃeɪndʒ], [iː diː aɪ]	elektronischer Datenaustausch
recognise (v)	[ˈrekəgnaɪz]	erkennen
trust (v)	[trʌst]	vertrauen
negotiable	[nɪˈgəʊʃiəbl]	übertragbar / begebbar
approve (v)	[əˈpruːv]	genehmigen
form	[fɔːm]	Formular
fill in / fill out (v)	[ˌfɪl ˈɪn], [ˌfɪl ˈaʊt]	ausfüllen
gift	[gɪft]	Geschenk
payment	[ˈpeɪmənt]	Bezahlung
export declaration	[ˈekspɔːt ˌdekləˈreɪʃən]	Ausfuhrerklärung
accompany (v)	[əˈkʌmpəni]	begleiten
consume (v)	[kənˈsjuːm]	verbrauchen
road waybill	[ˈrəʊd ˌweɪbɪl]	Frachtbrief
bill (duck's bill)	[bɪl], [ˈdʌks ˌbɪl]	(Enten)schnabel
consignor	[kənˈsaɪnə]	Versender
specimen	[ˈspesəmən]	Muster
multi-modal transport	[ˌmʌlti ˈməʊdəl ˌtrænspɔːt]	Kombiverkehr
consigned to the order of	[kənˈsaɪnd tu ði ˈɔːdər ɒf]	zur Verfügung von
notify address	[ˈnəʊtɪfaɪ əˈdres]	Meldeadresse
place of receipt	[ˌpleɪs ɒf rɪˈsiːt]	Übernahmeort
ocean vessel	[ˈəʊʃən ˌvesəl]	Seeschiff
port of loading	[ˌpɔːt ɒf ˈləʊdɪŋ]	Verschiffungshafen
port of discharge	[ˌpɔːt ɒf ˈdɪstʃɑːdʒ]	Löschhafen
place of delivery	[ˌpleɪs ɒf dɪˈlɪvəri]	Entladeort
place of issue	[ˌpleɪs ɒf ˈɪʃuː]	Ausstellungsort
date of issue	[ˌdeɪt ɒf ˈɪʃuː]	Austellungsdatum
stamp	[stæmp]	Stempel
signature	[ˈsɪgnətʃə]	Unterschrift
gross weight	[ˈgrəʊs ˌweɪt]	Bruttogewicht
standard conditions	[ˈstændəd kənˈdɪʃənz]	allgemeine Bedingungen
taken in charge in good order and condition	[ˈteɪkən ɪn ˌtʃɑːdʒ ɪn gʊd ˈɔːdər ænd kənˈdɪʃən]	übernommen in einwandfreiem Zustand
tick (v)	[tɪk]	mit einem Häkchen versehen
declaration	[ˌdekləˈreɪʃən]	Erklärung / Deklaration
clause	[klɔːz]	Klausel
be liable for (v)	[bi ˈlaɪəbl fɔː]	haften für
damage	[ˈdæmɪdʒ]	Beschädigung
delay	[dɪˈleɪ]	Verzögerung
declare (v) (value)	[dɪˈkleə (ˈvæljuː)]	angeben
clean bill of lading	[ˌkliːn ˈbɪl ɒf ˈleɪdɪŋ]	reines Konnossement
inadequate	[ɪnˈædɪkwət]	nicht ausreichend
apparent	[əˈpærənt]	scheinbar
short shipped	[ʃɔːt ʃɪpt]	fehlerhafte Teillieferung
drum	[drʌm]	Fässchen
leak (v)	[liːk]	auslaufen / lecken
good order	[ˌgʊd ˈɔːdə]	guter Zustand

non-negotiable	[ˌnɒnnɪˈɡəʊʃɪəbl]	nicht begebbar /nicht übertragbar
road haulier	[ˌrəʊd ˈhɔːliə]	Frachtführer
shipping note	[ˈʃɪpɪŋ ˌnəʊt]	Versandnote
waybill	[ˈweɪbɪl]	Frachtbrief
carrier	[ˈkærɪə]	Verkehrsträger
recipient	[rɪˈsɪpɪənt]	Empfänger
misuse (v)	[ˌmɪsˈjuːz]	falsch einsetzen
claim form	[ˈkleɪm ˌfɔːm]	Schadenersatzformular
policy	[ˈpɒləsi]	Police
claim	[kleɪm]	Schadenersatzanspruch
discovery	[dɪˈskʌvəri]	Entdeckung
insured (person)	[ɪnˈʃʊəd (ˈpɜːsən)]	Versicherte®
premium	[ˈpriːmɪəm]	Prämie
register (v)	[ˈredʒɪstə]	anmelden
bank account	[ˈbæŋk əˌkaʊnt]	Bankkonto
bank branch code	[bæŋk brɑːntʃ kəʊd]	Bankleitzahl
occur (v)	[əˈkɜː]	geschehen
pick up (v)	[ˌpɪk ˈʌp]	abholen
deliver (v)	[dɪˈlɪvə]	liefern
inspect (v)	[ɪnˈspekt]	inspizieren / prüfen
above	[əˈbʌv]	oben
convention	[kənˈvenʃən]	Konvention
documentary collection	[ˌdɒkjəˈmentəri kəˈlekʃən]	Dokumente gegen Zahlung
cash payment	[ˈkæʃ ˌpeɪmənt]	Barzahlung
in advance	[ˌɪn ədˈvɑːns]	im Voraus
irrevocable	[ɪrɪˈvəʊkəbl], [ɪˈrevəkəbl]	unwiderruflich

UNIT 8

space	[speɪs]	Raum
rack	[ræk]	Regal
pick (v) (goods in warehouse)	[pɪk (gʊdz ɪn ˈweəhaʊs)]	kommissionieren
kind	[kaɪnd]	Sorte
area	[ˈeərɪə]	Bereich
stock list / inventory	[ˈstɒk lɪst / ˈɪnvəntri / ɪnˈventəri]	Inventar
tick off (v)	[ˌtɪk ˈɒf]	abhaken
compare (v)	[kəmˈpeə]	vergleichen
floor	[flɔː]	Stockwerk
high-racking storage	[ˌhaɪˈrækɪŋ ˈstɔːrɪdʒ]	Hochregallager
conveyor belt	[kənˈveɪə ˌbelt]	Fließband
narrow	[ˈnærəʊ]	eng
gravity	[ˈɡrævəti]	Schwerkraft
delivery note	[dɪˈlɪvəri ˌnəʊt]	Lieferschein
in sight	[ˌɪn ˈsaɪt]	in Sicht
without a hitch	[wɪˌðaʊt ə ˈhɪtʃ]	reibungslos
in charge of	[ɪn ˈtʃɑːdʒ ɒf]	verantwortlich für
shelf (plural: shelves)	[ʃelf], [ʃelvz]	Regal
area	[ˈeərɪə]	Bereich
marshal (v)	[ˈmɑːʃəl]	bereitstellen / rangieren

lane	[leɪn]	Spur
dispatch	[dɪˈspætʃ]	Abfertigung / Versand
aisle	[aɪl]	Gang
profit margin	[ˈprɒfɪt ˌmɑːdʒɪn]	Gewinnspanne
replace (v)	[rɪˈpleɪs]	ersetzen
tag	[tæg]	Tag / Etikett
embed (v)	[ɪmˈbed]	einbetten
theft	[θeft]	Diebstahl
delivery note	[dɪˈlɪvəri ˌnəʊt]	Lieferschein
machinery	[məˈʃiːnəri]	Maschinen
in working order	[ˌɪn ˈwɜːkɪŋ ˈɔːdə]	betriebsbereit
outgoing goods	[ˌaʊtˈgəʊɪŋ ˌgʊdz]	Warenausgang
project leader	[ˈprɒdʒekt ˌliːdə]	Projektleiter(in)
agenda	[əˈdʒendə]	Tagesordnung
comply with (something)	[kəmˈplaɪ wɪð (ˌsʌmθɪŋ)]	sich nach etwas richten
package	[ˈpækɪdʒ]	Paket
standard	[ˈstændəd]	Norm
go-ahead	[ˈgəʊəhed]	grünes Licht
recommend (v)	[ˌrekəˈmend]	empfehlen
suitable	[ˈsuːtəbl], [ˈsjuːtəbl]	passend
firm	[fɜːm]	definitiv / eindeutig
recommendation	[ˌrekəmenˈdeɪʃən]	Empfehlung
agree (v)	[əˈgriː]	übereinstimmen / einverstanden sein
suggest (v)	[səˈdʒest]	vorschlagen
show (v)	[ʃəʊ]	zeigen
goods -in	[ˌgʊdzˈɪn]	Wareneingang
demonstrate (v)	[ˈdemənstreɪt]	demonstrieren
solution	[səˈluːʃən]	Lösung
point	[pɔɪnt]	Punkt
item	[ˈaɪtəm]	Punkt
participant	[pɑːˈtɪsɪpənt]	Teilnehmer(in)
liaison	[liˈeɪzən]	Zusammenarbeit
conduct (v)	[kənˈdʌkt]	führen
process	[ˈprəʊses]	Prozedur
hand over (v)	[ˌhænd ˈəʊvə]	übergeben / überreichen
report	[rɪˈpɔːt]	Bericht
minutes	[ˈmɪnɪts]	Protokoll
chairman	[ˈtʃeəmən]	Vorsitzende(r)
willing	[ˈwɪlɪŋ]	bereit
confident	[ˈkɒnfɪdənt]	sicher
module	[ˈmɒdjuːl]	Modul
cancel (v)	[ˈkænsəl]	stornieren
trial run	[ˈtraɪəl ˌrʌn]	Probelauf
variation	[ˌveəriˈeɪʃən]	Veränderung
map	[mæp]	Plan / Karte
incorrect	[ˈɪnkərekt]	nicht korrekt
in stock	[ˌɪn ˈstɒk]	auf Lager
out of stock	[ˌaʊt əf ˈstɒk]	ausverkauft

lose track (v)	[ˌluːz ˈtræk]	den Überblick verlieren
employed	[ɪmˈplɔɪd]	beschäftigt
short-term	[ˌʃɔːtˈtɜːm]	kurzfristig
hub	[hʌb]	Radnabe
spoke	[spəʊk]	Speiche
wheel	[wiːl]	Rad
dairy products	[ˈdeəri ˌprɒdʌkts]	Milchprodukte
cool chain	[ˈkuːl ˌtʃeɪn]	Kühlkette
ripen (v)	[ˈraɪpən]	reifen
treatment	[ˈtriːtmənt]	Behandlung
access	[ˈækses]	Zugriff / Zutritt
labelling	[ˈleɪbəlɪŋ]	Etikettierung
assembly	[əˈsembli]	Montage
palletiser	[ˈpælətaɪzə]	Palettierer
shrink-wrap (v)	[ˈʃrɪŋkræp]	einschweißen
crate	[kreɪt]	Kiste
carton	[ˈkɑːtən]	Karton
barrel	[ˈbærəl]	Fass
bale	[beɪl]	Ballen
sack	[sæk]	Sack
packaging	[ˈpækɪdʒɪŋ]	Verpackung
bottle	[ˈbɒtl]	abfüllen
bottling plant	[ˈbɒtlɪŋ ˌplɑːnt]	Abfüllanlage
labour	[ˈleɪbə]	Arbeitskraft

UNIT 9

military	[ˈmɪlɪtri]	militärisch
campaign	[kæmˈpeɪn]	Kampagne
troops	[truːps]	Truppen
supplies	[səˈplaɪz]	Vorräte
sense	[sens]	Bedeutung
is concerned with	[ɪz kənˈsɜːnd ˌwɪð]	beschäftigt sich mit
enterprise	[ˈentəpraɪz]	Firma / Unternehmen
react (v)	[riˈækt]	reagieren
contract logistics	[ˈkɒntrækt ləˈdʒɪstɪks]	Kontraktlogistik
outsourcing	[ˈaʊtsɔːsɪŋ]	Outsourcing
cost-effective	[ˌkɒstɪˈfektɪv]	kostengünstig
buffer	[ˈbʌfə]	Puffer
streamline (v)	[ˈstriːmlaɪn]	rationalisieren
site	[saɪt]	Platz
end user	[ˈend ˌjuːzə]	Endverbraucher
waste	[weɪst]	Abfall
disposal	[dɪˈspəʊzəl]	Beseitigung
sub-contractor	[ˌsʌbkənˈtræktə]	Subunternehmer
automotive industry	[ˌɔːtəˈməʊtɪv ˈɪndəstri]	Automobilindustrie
pharmaceutical industry	[ˌfɑːməˈsjuːtɪkəl ˈɪndəstri]	Pharmaindustrie
prescription	[prɪˈskrɪpʃən]	Rezept (vom Arzt)
customise (v)	[ˈkʌstəmaɪz]	anpassen / individualisieren
cider	[ˈsaɪdə]	Apfelwein

core	[kɔː]	Kern
rag	[ræg]	Lappen / Fetzen
ready-to-wear	['redi tu 'weə]	fertig zum Anziehen
hanger	['hæŋə]	Bügel
foil	[fɔɪl]	Folie
crease (v)	[kriːs]	zerknittern
response	[rɪ'spɒns]	Antwort / Reaktion
retail trade	['riːteɪl ˌtreɪd]	Einzelhandel
pull (v)	[pʊl]	ziehen
brand	[brænd]	Marke
soap	[səʊp]	Seife
make	[meɪk]	Marke
wind farm	['wɪnd ˌfɑːm]	Windpark
offshore	['ɒfʃɔː]	offshore / im Meer
fossil fuels	['fɒsəl 'fjuːəlz]	fossiler Brennstoff
scarce	[skeəs]	knapp
preserve (v)	[prɪ'zɜːv]	erhalten
environment	[ɪn'vaɪrənmənt]	Umwelt
carbon dioxide	['kɑːbən daɪ'ɒksaɪd]	Kohlendioxide
landscape	['lændskeɪp]	Landschaft
spoil (v)	[spɔɪl]	zerstören
turning blades	['tɜːnɪŋ ˌbleɪdz]	Rotorblätter
disturb (v)	[dɪ'stɜːb]	stören
nuclear power	['njuːkliə 'paʊə]	Kernkraft
resident	['rezɪdənt]	Einwohner
renewable	[rɪ'njuːəbl]	erneuerbar
key	[kiː]	Schlüssel
fair weather	[feə 'weðə]	schönes Wetter
enormous	[ɪ'nɔːməs]	gigantisch
lifting gear	['lɪftɪŋ ˌgɪə]	Hebezug
assemble (v)	[ə'sembl]	montieren
harbour (Am.Eng. harbor)	['hɑːbə]	Hafen
generator	['dʒenəreɪtə]	Generator
giant	['dʒaɪənt]	Riese

UNIT 10

personnel	[pɜːsə'nel]	Personal
consultant	[kən'sʌltənt]	Berater
salary	['sæləri]	Gehalt
client	['klaɪənt]	Kunde
branch	[brɑːntʃ]	Sukkursale / Filiale
ambitious	[æm'bɪʃəs]	ehrgeizig
degree	[dɪ'griː]	Diplom (Universität)
discipline	['dɪsəplɪn]	Fach
hands-on experience	[ˌhændz'ɒn ɪk'spɪərəns]	praktische Erfahrung
chance	[tʃɑːns]	Gelegenheit
fluent	['fluːənt]	fließend
curriculum vitae (CV)	[kəˌrɪkjələm 'viːtaɪ], [siː viː]	Lebenslauf
executive	[ɪg'zekjətɪv]	leitende(r) Angestellte(r)

in-company	[ˌɪnˈkʌmpəni]	im Betrieb
relationship	[rɪˈleɪʃənʃɪp]	Beziehung
warehouse operative	[ˈweəhaʊs ˈɒpərətɪv]	Lagerarbeiter(in)
implementation	[ˌɪmplɪmenˈteɪʃən]	Ausführung
key customer	[ˈkiː ˌkʌstəmə]	Schlüsselkunde / wichtiger Kunde
competitor	[kəmˈpetɪtə]	Konkurrenz
examination	[ɪgˌzæmɪˈneɪʃən]	Prüfung
occupation	[ˌɒkjəˈpeɪʃən]	Beschäftigung / Beruf
apply for (v) a job	[əˈplaɪ fɔːr ə dʒɒb]	sich bewerben
work placement	[ˈwɜːk ˌpleɪsmənt]	Praktikum
date of birth	[ˌdeɪt ɒf ˈbɜːθ]	Geburtsdatum
marital status	[ˈmærɪtəl ˈsteɪtəs]	Familienstand
native speaker	[ˈneɪtɪv ˌspiːkə]	Muttersprachler(in)
covering letter	[ˈkʌvərɪŋ ˌletə]	Anschreiben, Begleitbrief
post	[pəʊst]	Stelle
advertised	[ˈædvətaɪzd]	ausgeschrieben
enclosed	[ɪnˈkləʊzd]	beigefügt
testimonial	[ˌtestɪˈməʊniəl]	Zeugnis
on request	[ˌɒn rɪˈkwest]	auf Wunsch
recognised	[ˈrekəgnaɪzd]	anerkannt
assure (v)	[əˈʃʊə]	versichern
course	[kɔːs]	Kursus
keen	[kiːn]	eifrig
goal	[gəʊl]	Ziel
staying power	[ˈsteɪɪŋ ˌpaʊə]	Durchhaltevermögen
apprenticeship	[əˈprentɪsʃɪp]	einstellen
recruit (v)	[rɪˈkruːt]	Lehre / Lehrzeit
task	[tɑːsk]	Aufgabe
join (v) a company	[dʒɔɪn (ə ˈkʌmpəni)]	anfangen, bei einer Firma zu arbeiten
interviewer	[ˈɪntəvjuːə]	Leiter des Vorstellungsgespräch
period of notice	[ˈpɪəriəd ɒf ˈnəʊtɪs]	Kündigungsfrist
quarter	[ˈkwɔːtə]	Quartal
Interview (for a job)	[ˈɪntəvjuː (fɔːr ə dʒɒb)]	Vorstellungsgespräch
temporary job	[ˌtempərəri ˈdʒɒb]	Aushilfsstelle
finals (final examinations)	[ˈfaɪnəlz (ˌfaɪnəl ɪgzæmɪˈneɪʃənz)]	Abschlußprüfung
impression	[ɪmˈpreʃən]	Eindruck
assess (v)	[əˈses]	einschätzen
get (v) used to (something)	[get ˈjuːzd tu (ˌsʌmθɪŋ)]	sich gewöhnen an (etwas)
convince (v)	[kənˈvɪns]	überzeugen
stage	[steɪdʒ]	Stadium
look after (v)	[ˌlʊk ˈɑːftər]	sich kümmern um
challenge	[ˈtʃæləndʒ]	Herausforderung
trade	[treɪd]	Handwerk

ADVANCED READING

board of directors	[bɔːd ɒf dɪˈrektəz]	Vorstand
persuade (v)	[pəˈsweɪd]	überzeugen
proceedings	[prəˈsiːdɪŋz]	Verfahren
trip	[trɪp]	Fahrt
figures	[ˈfɪgəz]	Zahlen
appendix	[əˈpendɪks]	Anhang
domestic sales	[dəˈmestɪk ˌseɪlz]	Inlandsumsatz
lead (v)	[liːd]	führen
process an order (v)	[ˈprəʊses ən ˈɔːdə]	einen Auftrag ausführen
range	[reɪndʒ]	Palette / Assortiment
replenish (v)	[rɪˈplenɪʃ]	wieder auffüllen
plant	[plɑːnt]	Werk
run	[rʌn]	Fahrt
loading capacity	[ˈləʊdɪŋ kəˈpæsəti]	Ladekapazität
outsource (v)	[ˈaʊtsɔːs]	outsourcen/ auslagern
joint initiative	[ˌdʒɔɪnt ɪˈnɪʃətɪv]	gemeinsame Initiative
integrity	[ɪnˈtegrəti]	Integrität
participate (v)	[pɑːˈtɪsɪpeɪt]	teilnehmen
encompass (v)	[ɪnˈkʌmpəs]	umfassen
access controls	[ˈækses kənˌtrəʊlz]	Zugangskontrollen
manifest procedure	[ˈmænɪfest prəˈsiːdʒə]	Ladelisteverfahren
questionnaire	[ˌkwestʃəˈneə]	Fragebogen
benefit	[ˈbenəfɪt]	Vorteil
eligibility	[ˌelɪdʒəˈbɪləti]	Berechtigung
emphasis	[ˈemfəsɪs]	Betonung
terrorism	[ˈterərɪzm]	Terrorismus
enhance (v)	[ɪnˈhɑːns]	verbessern

Vocabulary (alphabetical order)

a

above	[əˈbʌv]	oben
abroad	[əˈbrɔːd]	Ausland
accept (v)	[əkˈsept]	akzeptieren
acceptable	[əkˈseptəbl]	annehmbar
access	[ˈækses]	Zugriff / Zutritt
access controls	[ˈækses kənˌtrəʊlz]	Zugangskontrollen
accidentally	[ˌæksɪˈdentəli]	ohne Absicht
accompany (v)	[əˈkʌmpəni]	begleiten
according to	[əˈkɔːdɪŋ tu]	gemäß
adhesive	[ədˈhiːsɪv]	haftend / Haft-
advertise (v)	[ˈædvətaɪz]	Werbung machen für
advertised	[ˈædvətaɪzd]	ausgeschrieben
advise (v)	[ədˈvaɪz]	beraten
agenda	[əˈdʒendə]	Tagesordnung
agree (v)	[əˈgriː]	übereinstimmen / einverstanden sein
agreement	[əˈgriːmənt]	Abmachung
agricultural product	[ˌægrɪˈkʌltʃərəl ˌprɒdʌkts]	landwirtschaftliche Produkte
air waybill	[ˈeə ˌweɪbɪl]	Luftfrachtbrief
airfreight	[ˈeəfreɪt]	Luftfracht
aisle	[aɪl]	Gang
allocate (v)	[ˈæləkeɪt]	zuteilen
allowed	[əˈlaʊd]	erlaubt
altogether	[ˌɔːltəˈgeðə]	insgesamt
ambitious	[æmˈbɪʃəs]	ehrgeizig
amount	[əˈmaʊnt]	Menge
annually	[ˈænjuəli]	jährlich
apologise (v)	[əˈpɒlədʒaɪz]	sich entschuldigen
apparent	[əˈpærənt]	scheinbar
appendix	[əˈpendɪks]	Anhang
applicant	[ˈæplɪkənt]	Bewerber(in)
apply for (v) a job	[əˈplaɪ fɔːr ə dʒɒb]	sich bewerben
appointment	[əˈpɔɪntmənt]	Termin
apprenticeship	[əˈprentɪsʃɪp]	einstellen
approve (v)	[əˈpruːv]	genehmigen
approximate	[əˈprɒksɪmət]	ungefähr
approximately	[əˈprɒksɪmətli]	circa / zirka
archive (v)	[ˈɑːkaɪv]	archivieren
area	[ˈeərɪə]	Fläche / Bereich
arouse (v)	[əˈraʊz]	erwecken
arrival	[əˈraɪvəl]	Ankunft
article number	[ˈɑːtɪkl ˌnʌmbə]	Artikelnummer
ASAP = as soon as possible	[eɪ es eɪ piː], [æz suːn æz ˈpɒsəbl]	so bald wie möglich
assemble (v)	[əˈsembl]	montieren
assembly	[əˈsembli]	Montage

assembly line	[əˈsembli ˌlaɪn]	Montageband
assess (v)	[əˈses]	einschätzen
assure (v)	[əˈʃʊə]	versichern
asterisk	[ˈæstərɪsk]	Sternchen
attached	[əˈtætʃt]	im Anhang
attached file	[əˌtætʃt ˈfaɪl]	Anhang
authority	[ɔːˈɒrəti]	Behörde
automotive company	[ˌɔːtəˈməʊtɪv ˌkʌmpəni]	Autohersteller
automotive industry	[ˌɔːtəˈməʊtɪv ˈɪndəstri]	Automobilindustrie
availability	[əˌveɪləˈbɪləti]	Verfügbarkeit
available	[əˈveɪləbl]	verfügbar
avoid (v)	[əˈvɔɪd]	vermeiden

b

back order	[ˌbæk ˈɔːdə]	nicht gelieferte Bestellung
backlog	[ˈbæklɒg]	Auftragsrückstand
balance of trade	[ˌbæləns ɒf ˈtreɪd]	Handelsbilanz
bale	[beɪl]	Ballen
bank account	[ˈbæŋk əˌkaʊnt]	Bankkonto
bank branch code	[bæŋk brɑːntʃ kəʊd]	Bankleitzahl
barcode	[ˈbɑːkəʊd]	Strichcode
barge	[bɑːdʒ]	Kahn
barrel	[ˈbærəl]	Fass
be able to (v)	[bɪ ˈeɪbl tu]	können
be liable for (v)	[bi ˈlaɪəbl fɔː]	haften für
be lucky (v)	[bɪ ˈlʌki]	Glück haben
benefit	[ˈbenəfɪt]	Vorteil
berth	[bɜːθ]	Anlegeplatz
bill (duck's bill)	[bɪl], [ˈdʌks ˌbɪl]	(Enten)schnabel
bill of lading (B/L)	[ˌbɪl ɒf ˈleɪdɪŋ], [biː el]	Konnossement / Frachtbrief
binding	[ˈbaɪndɪŋ]	verbindlich
bleach	[bliːtʃ]	Bleichmittel
bleach (v)	[bliːtʃ]	bleichen
board	[bɔːd]	Brett
board of directors	[bɔːd ɒf dɪˈrektəz]	Vorstand
bonded store	[ˌbɒndɪd ˈstɔː]	Zolllager
book (v)	[bʊk]	buchen / reservieren
boring	[ˈbɔːrɪŋ]	langweilig
Bother!	[ˈbɒðə]	Verflixt!
bottle	[ˈbɒtl]	abfüllen
bottling plant	[ˈbɒtlɪŋ ˌplɑːnt]	Abfüllanlage
box	[bɒks]	Kiste
branch	[brɑːntʃ]	Sukkursale / Filiale
brand	[brænd]	Marke
breadth	[bredθ]	Breite
break	[breɪk]	Pause
break-bulk	[ˈbreɪkbʌlk]	Stückgut
broad	[brɔːd]	breit
buffer	[ˈbʌfə]	Puffer

bulk cargo	[ˈbʌlk ˌkɑːgəʊ]	Massengut
button	[ˈbʌtən]	Knopf

C

calculate (v)	[ˈkælkjəleɪt]	kalkulieren
caller	[ˈkɔːlə]	Anrufer
campaign	[kæmˈpeɪn]	Kampagne
canal	[kəˈnæl]	Kanal
cancel (v)	[ˈkænsəl]	stornieren
carbon dioxide	[ˈkɑːbən daɪˈɒksaɪd]	Kohlendioxide
cargo	[ˈkɑːgəʊ]	Fracht
cargo handling dues	[ˈkɑːgəʊ ˈhændlɪŋ ˌdjuːz]	Umschlagsgebühren
carpet	[ˈkɑːpɪt]	Teppich
carrier	[ˈkæriə]	Verkehrsträger
carton	[ˈkɑːtən]	Karton
cash payment	[ˈkæʃ ˌpeɪmənt]	Barzahlung
catchment area	[ˈkætʃmənt ˌeəriə]	Einzugsgebiet
cell	[sel]	Zelle
cell phone (USA)	[ˈsel ˌfəʊn]	Handy
cement	[sɪˈment]	Zement
centre of gravity	[ˈsentər ɒf ˈgrævəti]	Schwerpunkt
century	[ˈsentʃəri]	Jahrhundert
certificate of origin	[səˈtɪfɪkət ɒf ˈɒrɪdʒɪn]	Ursprungszeugnis
chain	[tʃeɪn]	Kette
chairman	[ˈtʃeəmən]	Vorsitzende(r)
challenge	[ˈtʃæləndʒ]	Herausforderung
chance	[tʃɑːns]	Gelegenheit
change	[tʃeɪndʒ]	Änderung
change (v)	[tʃeɪndʒ]	ändern
channel	[ˈtʃænəl]	Kanal
charge (v)	[tʃɑːdʒ]	berechnen
chart (v)	[tʃɑːt]	kartographisch erfassen
check (v)	[tʃek]	überprüfen
chemistry	[ˈkemɪstri]	Chemie
cider	[ˈsaɪdə]	Apfelwein
claim	[kleɪm]	Schadenersatzanspruch
claim form	[ˈkleɪm ˌfɔːm]	Schadenersatzformular
classify (v)	[ˈklæsɪfaɪ]	klassifizieren
clause	[klɔːz]	Klausel
clean bill of lading	[ˌkliːn ˈbɪl ɒf ˈleɪdɪŋ]	reines Konnossement
clear (v) (through customs)	[klɪə (θruː ˈkʌstəmz)]	abfertigen
client	[ˈklaɪənt]	Kunde
coal	[kəʊl]	Kohle
commercial invoice	[kəˈmɜːʃəl ˈɪnvɔɪs]	Handelsrechnung
commodity	[kəˈmɒdəti]	Ware
compare (v)	[kəmˈpeə]	vergleichen
compete (v)	[kəmˈpiːt]	konkurrieren
competitor	[kəmˈpetɪtə]	Konkurrenz
complain (v)	[kəmˈpleɪn]	sich beschweren

complaint	[kəmˈpleɪnt]	Beschwerde
comply with (something)	[kəmˈplaɪ wɪð (ˌsʌmθɪŋ)]	sich nach etwas richten
comply with (v)	[kəmˈplaɪ ˌwɪð]	einhalten
component	[kəmˈpəʊnənt]	Komponente
compressed	[kəmˈprest]	komprimiert
conduct (v)	[kənˈdʌkt]	führen
Conference lines	[ˈkɒnfərəns ˌlaɪnz]	Konferenzlinien
confident	[ˈkɒnfɪdənt]	sicher
confidentiality	[ˌkɒnfɪdenʃiˈæləti]	Vertraulichkeit
configure (v)	[kənˈfɪgə]	konfigurieren
confirm (v)	[kənˈfɜːm]	bestätigen
confirmation	[ˌkɒnfəˈmeɪʃən]	Bestätigung
congestion zone	[kənˈdʒestʃən ˌzəʊn]	Stauzone
connect (v)	[kəˈnekt]	verbinden
connected	[kəˈnektɪd]	verbunden
consigned to the order of	[kənˈsaɪnd tu ði ˈɔːdər ɒf]	zur Verfügung von
consignment	[kənˈsaɪnmənt]	Sendung
consignor	[kənˈsaɪnə]	Versender
consist of (v)	[kənˈsɪst ɒf]	bestehen aus
consolidation agent	[kənˌsɒlɪˈdeɪʃən ˌeɪdʒənt]	Sammelgutspediteur
consultant	[kənˈsʌltənt]	Berater
consume (v)	[kənˈsjuːm]	verbrauchen
consumer	[kənˈsjuːmə]	Verbraucher(in)
container-ship	[kənˈteɪnə ˌʃɪp]	Containerschiff
contents	[ˈkɒntents]	Inhalt
contract	[ˈkɒntrækt]	Vertrag
contract logistics	[ˈkɒntrækt ləˈdʒɪstɪks]	Kontraktlogistik
convention	[kənˈventʃən]	Konvention
conventional cargo	[kənˈventʃənəl ˈkɑːgəʊ]	konventionelle Ladung
conveyor belt	[kənˈveɪə ˌbelt]	Fließband
convince (v)	[kənˈvɪns]	überzeugen
cool (v)	[kuːl]	kühlen
cool chain	[ˈkuːl ˌtʃeɪn]	Kühlkette
cool-chain	[ˈkuːltʃeɪn]	Kühlkette
co-operate (v)	[kəʊˈɒpəreɪt]	kooperieren
co-operation	[kəʊˌɒpəˈreɪʃən]	Zusammenarbeit
copy	[ˈkɒpi]	Kopie
core	[kɔː]	Kern
corrosive	[kəˈrəʊsɪv]	korrosiv
cost-effective	[ˌkɒstɪˈfektɪv]	kostengünstig
costs	[kɒsts]	Kosten
course	[kɔːs]	Kursus
covering letter	[ˈkʌvərɪŋ ˌletə]	Anschreiben, Begleitbrief
crate	[kreɪt]	Kiste
crease (v)	[kriːs]	zerknittern
create (v)	[kriˈeɪt]	erzeugen
crew	[kruː]	Mannschaft
crude oil	[ˈkruːd ˌɔɪl]	Rohöl
cruise ship	[ˈkruːz ˌʃɪp]	Kreuzfahrtschiff

currency	['kʌrənsi]	Währung
curriculum vitae (CV)	[kə,rɪkjələm 'viːtaɪ], [siː viː]	Lebenslauf
custom	['kʌstəm]	Kundschaft
customer	['kʌstəmə]	Kunde
customise (v)	['kʌstəmaɪz]	anpassen / individualisieren
customised	['kʌstəmaɪzd]	auf Kundenwunsch gefertigt
customs	['kʌstəmz]	Zoll
customs officer	['kʌstəmz ,ɒfɪsə]	Zollbeamter
cut flowers	[,kʌt 'flaʊəz]	Schnittblumen

d

dairy products	['deəri ,prɒdʌkts]	Milchprodukte
damage	['dæmɪdʒ]	Schaden
damage (v)	['dæmɪdʒ]	beschädigen
damp	[dæmp]	Feuchtigkeit
danger	['deɪndʒə]	Gefahr
dangerous	['deɪndʒərəs]	gefährlich
date of birth	[,deɪt ɒf 'bɜːθ]	Geburtsdatum
date of issue	[,deɪt ɒf 'ɪʃuː]	Austellungsdatum
deal with (v)	['diːl ,wɪð]	sich kümmern um
decade	['dekeɪd]	Jahrzehnt
decide (v)	[dɪ'saɪd]	entscheiden
decision	[dɪ'sɪʒən]	Entscheidung
deck	[dek]	Deck
declaration	[,deklə'reɪʃən]	Erklärung / Deklaration
declare (v)	[dɪ'kleə]	deklarieren
declare (v) (value)	[dɪ'kleə ('væljuː)]	angeben
deep	[diːp]	tief
degree	[dɪ'griː]	Diplom (Universität)
delay	[dɪ'leɪ]	Verspätung
deliver (v)	[dɪ'lɪvə]	liefern
delivery	[dɪ'lɪvəri]	Lieferung
delivery note	[dɪ'lɪvəri ,nəʊt]	Lieferschein
delivery van	[dɪ'lɪvəri ,væn]	Lieferwagen
demonstrate (v)	['demənstreɪt]	demonstrieren
departure	[dɪ'pɑːtʃə]	Abfahrt / Abflug
depend on (v)	[dɪ'pend ,ɒn]	abhängen von
depth	[depθ]	Tiefe
describe (v)	[dɪ'skraɪb]	beschreiben
description	[dɪ'skrɪpʃən]	Beschreibung
designate (v)	['dezɪgneɪt]	designieren
destination	[destɪ'neɪʃən]	Bestimmungsort
develop (v)	[dɪ'veləp]	entwickeln
development	[dɪ'veləpmənt]	Entwicklung
dialling code	['daɪəlɪŋ ,kəʊd]	Vorwahl
dictated	[dɪk'teɪtɪd]	diktiert / entschieden
digit	['dɪdʒɪt]	Zahl
discipline	['dɪsəplɪn]	Fach
discovery	[dɪ'skʌvəri]	Entdeckung

disease	[dɪˈziːz]	Krankheit
dispatch	[dɪˈspætʃ]	Abfertigung / Versand
dispatch (v)	[dɪˈspætʃ]	versenden
disposal	[dɪˈspəʊzəl]	Beseitigung
distance	[ˈdɪstəns]	Entfernung
distributing company	[dɪˈstrɪbjuːtɪŋ ˈkʌmpəni]	Vertriebsgesellschaft
distribution	[ˌdɪstrɪˈbjuːʃən]	Vertrieb
distribution (department)	[ˌdɪstrɪˈbjuːʃən (dɪˈpɑːtmənt)]	Vertrieb(sabteilung)
disturb (v)	[dɪˈstɜːb]	stören
diversify (v)	[daɪˈvɜːsɪfaɪ]	diversifizieren
divided	[dɪˈvaɪdɪd]	geteilt
do sport (v)	[ˌduː ˈspɔːt]	Sport machen
dock worker	[ˈdɒk ˌwɜːkə]	Hafenarbeiter
document	[ˈdɒkjəmənt]	Papier / Dokument
documentary collection	[ˌdɒkjəˈmentəri kəˈlekʃən]	Dokumente gegen Zahlung
domestic	[dəˈmestɪk]	einheimisch
domestic sales	[dəˈmestɪk ˌseɪlz]	Inlandsumsatz
double-stack car	[ˈdʌblstæk ˌkɑː]	Doppelstock-Containerwagen
draught (of a ship)	[drɑːft (ɒf ə ʃɪp)]	Tiefgang
dream	[driːm]	Traum
drum	[drʌm]	Fässchen
dry	[draɪ]	trocken
durable	[ˈdjʊərəbl]	unverwüstlich
dutiable	[ˈdjuːtiəbl], [ˈdʒuː-]	zu verzollen
duty (customs duty)	[ˈdjuːti (ˈkʌstəmz ˌdjuːti)]	Zollabgabe

e

earn (v)	[ɜːn]	verdienen
economic	[iːkəˈnɒmɪk]	wirtschaftlich
electronic data interchange EDI	[ˌelekˈtrɒnɪk ˈdeɪtə ˈɪntətʃeɪndʒ], [iː diː aɪ]	elektronischer Datenaustausch
eligibility	[ˌelɪdʒəˈbɪləti]	Berechtigung
embed (v)	[ɪmˈbed]	einbetten
emit (v)	[ɪˈmɪt]	ausstoßen
emphasis	[ˈemfəsɪs]	Betonung
employed	[ɪmˈplɔɪd]	beschäftigt
employee	[ɪmˈplɔɪiː], [ˌemplɔɪˈiː]	Arbeitnehmer(in)
enclosed	[ɪnˈkləʊzd]	beigefügt
encompass (v)	[ɪnˈkʌmpəs]	umfassen
end user	[ˈend ˌjuːzə]	Endverbraucher
endanger (v)	[ɪnˈdeɪndʒə]	gefährden
enhance (v)	[ɪnˈhɑːns]	verbessern
enormous	[ɪˈnɔːməs]	gigantisch
enquiry	[ɪnˈkwaɪəri]	Anfrage
ensure (v)	[ɪnˈʃɔː], [-ˈʃʊə]	versichern
enterprise	[ˈentəpraɪz]	Firma / Unternehmen
environment	[ɪnˈvaɪrənmənt]	Umwelt
equipment	[ɪˈkwɪpmənt]	Ausstattung / Bedarf

examination	[ɪgˌzæmɪ'neɪʃən]	Prüfung
excited	[ɪk'saɪtɪd]	aufgeregt
executive	[ɪg'zekjətɪv]	leitende(r) Angestellte(r)
exhaust gas	[ɪg'zɔːst ˌgæs]	Abgase
exhibit (v)	[ɪg'zɪbɪt]	ausstellen
expand (v)	[ɪk'spænd]	expandieren
expectation	[ˌekspek'teɪʃən]	Erwartung
experienced	[ɪk'spɪərɪənst]	erfahren
explanation	[ˌeksplə'neɪʃən]	Erklärung
explosive	[ɪk'spləʊsɪv]	Sprengstoff / explosiv
export declaration	['ekspɔːt ˌdeklə'reɪʃən]	Ausfuhrerklärung
extension number	[ɪk'stenʃən ˌnʌmbə]	Durchwahl

f

facilities	[fə'sɪlətiz]	Anlagen
fair weather	[feə 'weðə]	schönes Wetter
favour	['feɪvə]	Bitte
feeder service	['fiːdə ˌsɜːvɪs]	Zubringerdienst
ferry	['feri]	Fähre
fewer	['fjuːə]	weniger
figures	['fɪgəz]	Zahlen
file	[faɪl]	Datei
fill in / fill out (v)	[ˌfɪl 'ɪn], [ˌfɪl 'aʊt]	ausfüllen
final total	['faɪnəl 'təʊtəl]	Endsumme
finals (final examinations)	['faɪnəlz (ˌfaɪnəl ɪgzæmɪ'neɪʃənz)]	Abschlußprüfung
fine	[faɪn]	Bußgeld
finished product	['fɪnɪʃt 'prɒdʌkt]	Fertigprodukt
firm	[fɜːm]	fest
flammable	['flæməbl]	feuergefährlich
float (v)	[fləʊt]	schwimmen
flock	[flɒk]	Schwarm
floor	[flɔː]	Stockwerk
flotsam	['flɒtsəm]	Strandgut
fluent	['fluːənt]	fließend
foil	[fɔɪl]	Folie
footwear	['fʊtweə]	Schuhe
forbidden	[fə'bɪdən]	verboten
foreseeable	[fɔː'siːəbl]	vorhersehbar
fork-lift truck	[ˌfɔːklɪft 'trʌk]	Gabelstapler
form	[fɔːm]	Formular
fossil fuels	['fɒsəl 'fjuːəlz]	fossiler Brennstoff
found (v)	[faʊnd]	begründen / gründen
fragile	['frædʒaɪl]	zerbrechlich
freight forwarder	['freɪt ˌfɔːwədə]	Spediteur
fuel	['fjuːəl]	Brennstoff
function (v)	['fʌŋkʃən]	funktionieren
furniture	['fɜːnɪtʃə]	Möbeln

g

gantry crane	[ˈgæntrɪ ˌkreɪn]	Portalkran
gap	[gæp]	Lücke
garment	[ˈgɑːmənt]	Kleidungsstück
gas station (US), petrol station (GB)	[ˈgæs ˌsteɪʃən], [ˈpetrəl ˌsteɪʃən]	Tankstelle
gasket	[ˈgæskɪt]	Dichtung
gauge	[geɪdʒ]	Spurbreite
generator	[ˈdʒenəreɪtə]	Generator
get (v) used to (something)	[get ˈjuːzd tu (ˌsʌmθɪŋ)]	sich gewöhnen an (etwas)
giant	[ˈdʒaɪənt]	Riese
gift	[gɪft]	Geschenk
go on (v)	[ˌgəʊ ˈɒn]	weiter machen / weiter sprechen
go-ahead	[ˈgəʊəhed]	grünes Licht
goal	[gəʊl]	Ziel
good order	[ˌgʊd ˈɔːdə]	guter Zustand
goods	[gʊdz]	Güter / Waren
goods -in	[ˌgʊdzˈɪn]	Wareneingang
goods train	[ˈgʊdz ˌtreɪn]	Güterzug
grain	[greɪn]	Korn
gravity	[ˈgrævəti]	Schwerkraft
gross weight	[ˈgrəʊs ˌweɪt]	Bruttogewicht
groupage container	[ˈgruːpɪdʒ kənˌteɪnə]	Sammelcontainer
gym	[dʒɪm]	Fitnesscenter / Turnhalle

h

hair-net	[ˈheənet]	Haarnetz
hand over (v)	[ˌhænd ˈəʊvə]	übergeben / überreichen
handle (v) (freight)	[ˈhændl (freɪt)]	umschlagen (Fracht)
handling	[ˈhændlɪŋ]	Umschlag
hands-on experience	[ˌhændzˈɒn ɪkˈspɪərəns]	praktische Erfahrung
Hang on a minute!	[hæŋ ˈɒn ə ˌmɪnɪt]	Warten Sie einen Moment!
hang up (v) (on phone)	[ˌhæŋ ˈʌp (ɒn fəʊn)]	auflegen / ein Telefonat beenden
hanger	[ˈhæŋə]	Bügel
hanging rail	[ˈhæŋɪŋ ˌreɪl]	Kleiderbügelhalter
happen (v)	[ˈhæpən]	passieren
harbour (Am.Eng. harbor)	[ˈhɑːbə]	Hafen
hazardous	[ˈhæzədəs]	gefährlich
hazardous goods	[ˈhæzədəs ˌgʊdz]	Gefahrgut
head of department	[ˌhed ɒf dɪˈpɑːtmənt]	Abteilungsleiter (-in)
headquarters	[ˈhedkwɔːtəz]	Hauptquartier / Hauptsitz
health	[helθ]	Gesundheit
heat	[hiːt]	Hitze
heavy goods vehicle / lorry / truck	[ˌhevi ˈgʊdz ˌvɪəkl / ˈlɒri / trʌk]	Lastwagen
heavy-weight	[ˈheviweɪt]	Schwergewicht
height	[haɪt]	Höhe
high	[haɪ]	hoch
high-racking storage	[ˌhaɪˈrækɪŋ ˈstɔːrɪdʒ]	Hochregallager

hold	[həʊld]	Frachtraum
hopper	['hɒpə]	Klappdeck
hopper car	['hɒpə ˌkɑː]	Klappdeckelwagen
household goods	['haʊshəʊld ˌgʊdz]	Haushaltsgüte
hub	[hʌb]	Radnabe
hygiene	['haɪdʒiːn]	Hygiene

i

I'll put you on hold.	[aɪl 'pʊt ju ɒn 'həʊld]	Ich setze Sie in die Warteschlange.
ice	[aɪs]	Eis
if it's not too much trouble	[ɪf ɪts nɒt tuː mʌtʃ 'trʌbl]	wenn es Ihnen nicht zu viel ausmacht
imagine (v)	[ɪ'mædʒɪn]	sich vorstellen
implementation	[ˌɪmplɪmen'teɪʃən]	Ausführung
impression	[ɪm'preʃən]	Eindruck
in addition	[ˌɪn ə'dɪʃən]	zusätzlich
in advance	[ˌɪn əd'vɑːns]	im Voraus
in charge of	[ɪn 'tʃɑːdʒ ɒf]	verantwortlich für
in demand	[ˌɪn dɪ'mɑːnd]	gefragt
in good condition	[ɪn gʊd kən'dɪʃən]	in gutem Zustand
in sight	[ˌɪn 'saɪt]	in Sicht
in stock	[ˌɪn 'stɒk]	auf Lager
in transit	[ˌɪn 'trænsɪt]	auf der Durchreise
in working order	[ˌɪn 'wɜːkɪŋ 'ɔːdə]	betriebsbereit
inadequate	[ɪn'ædɪkwət]	nicht ausreichend
included	[ɪn'kluːdɪd]	einbeschlossen
in-company	[ˌɪn'kʌmpəni]	im Betrieb
incorrect	['ɪnkərekt]	nicht korrekt
increase (v)	[ɪn'kriːs]	zunehmen / steigern
inevitable	[ɪ'nevɪtəbl]	unvermeidlich
inland waterways	['ɪnlænd 'wɔːtəweɪz]	Binnengewässer
inspect (v)	[ɪn'spekt]	inspizieren / prüfen
inspection authority	[ɪn'spekʃən ɔː'θɒrəti]	Prüfstelle
inspector	[ɪn'spektə]	Inspektor
instead of	[ɪn'sted ˌɒf]	anstatt
instructions	[ɪn'strʌkʃənz]	Anleitung
insulate	['ɪnsjəleɪt]	isoliert
insulate (v)	['ɪnsjəleɪt]	isolieren
insurance	[ɪn'ʃʊərəns]	Versicherung
insurance premium	[ɪn'ʃʊərəns ˌpriːmiəm]	Versicherungsprämie
insured (person)	[ɪn'ʃʊəd ('pɜːsən)]	Versicherte®
integrity	[ɪn'tegrəti]	Integrität
interface (v)	['ɪntəfeɪs]	Schnittstelle / Interface
internship / work placement	['ɪntɜːnʃɪp], ['wɜːk ˌpleɪsmənt]	Praktikum
Interview (for a job)	['ɪntəvjuː (fɔːr ə dʒɒb)]	Vorstellungsgespräch
interviewer	['ɪntəvjuːə]	Leiter des Vorstellungsgespräch
introduce (yourself) (v)	['ɪntrədjuːs (jɔː'self)]	sich melden
inventory	['ɪnvəntri], [ɪn'ventəri]	Inventar

invoice	['ɪnvɔɪs]	Rechnung
invoice (v)	['ɪnvɔɪs]	berechnen
iron ore	['aɪən ˌɔː]	Eisenerz
irrevocable	[ɪrɪ'vəʊkəbl], [ɪ'revəkəbl]	unwiderruflich
is concerned with	[ɪz kən'sɜːnd ˌwɪð]	beschäftigt sich mit
issue (v) (a document)	['ɪʃuː (ə 'dɒkjəmənt)]	ausstellen
It would be worthwhile.	[ɪt wʊd bi 'wɜːθwaɪl]	Es würde sich lohnen.
item	['aɪtəm]	Punkt

j

job	[dʒɒb]	Aufgabe/ Arbeitsstelle
join (v) a company	[dʒɔɪn (ə 'kʌmpəni)]	anfangen, bei einer Firma zu arbeiten
joint initiative	[ˌdʒɔɪnt ɪ'nɪʃətɪv]	gemeinsame Initiative
joke	[dʒəʊk]	Witz

k

keen	[kiːn]	eifrig
key	[kiː]	Schlüssel
key customer	['kiː ˌkʌstəmə]	Schlüsselkunde / wichtiger Kunde
kind	[kaɪnd]	Sorte

l

label	['leɪbəl]	Etikett
labelling	['leɪbəlɪŋ]	Etikettierung
labour	['leɪbə]	Arbeitskraft
landing gear	['lændɪŋ ˌgɪə]	Fahrgestell
landscape	['lændskeɪp]	Landschaft
lane	[leɪn]	Spur
launch (v)	[lɔːntʃ]	einführen
law	[lɔː]	Gesetz
lead (v)	[liːd]	führen
leak (v)	[liːk]	auslaufen / lecken
length	[leŋθ]	Länge
letter of credit (L/C)	['letər ɒf 'kredɪt], [el siː]	Akkreditiv
liaison	[li'eɪzən]	Zusammenarbeit
lift (v)	[lɪft]	heben
lifting gear	['lɪftɪŋ ˌgɪə]	Hebezug
lighter	['laɪtə]	leichter
live animals	[ˌlaɪv 'ænɪməlz]	lebende Tiere
load	[ləʊd]	Ladung
load (v)	[ləʊd]	laden
loading aid	['ləʊdɪŋ ˌeɪd]	Lademittel
loading capacity	['ləʊdɪŋ kə'pæsəti]	Ladekapazität
local	['ləʊkəl]	örtlich
lock (v)	[lɒk]	verriegeln / verschließen
log (v)	[lɒg]	protokollieren
long	[lɒŋ]	lang
look after (v)	[ˌlʊk 'ɑːftər]	sich kümmern um

loose	[luːs]	unverpackt
lose (v)	[luːz]	verlieren
lose track (v)	[ˌluːz ˈtræk]	den Überblick verlieren
loss	[lɒs]	Verlust
luckily	[ˈlʌkɪli]	glücklicherweise

m

machinery	[məˈʃiːnəri]	Maschinen
main road	[ˈmeɪn ˌrəʊd]	Hauptstraße
main task	[ˈmeɪn ˌtɑːsk]	Hauptaufgabe
mainland	[ˈmeɪnlænd]	Festland
maintain (v)	[meɪnˈteɪn]	erhalten
maintenance	[ˈmeɪntənəns]	Instandhaltung
make	[meɪk]	Marke
manage to do something	[ˈmænɪdʒ tu ˈduː ˌsʌmθɪŋ]	etwas schaffen
manifest / cargo list	[ˈmænɪfest / ˈkɑːgəʊ ˌlɪst]	Ladeliste
manifest procedure	[ˈmænɪfest prəˈsiːdʒə]	Ladelisteverfahren
manually	[ˈmænjuəli]	manuell
manufacture (v)	[ˌmænjəˈfæktʃə]	herstellen
manufacturer	[ˌmænjəˈfæktʃərə]	Hersteller
map	[mæp]	Plan / Karte
marital status	[ˈmærɪtəl ˈsteɪtəs]	Familienstand
maritime transport	[ˈmærɪtaɪm ˈtrænspɔːt]	Seetransport
mark	[mɑːk]	Markierung
mark (v)	[mɑːk]	markieren / kennzeichnen
marshal (v)	[ˈmɑːʃəl]	bereitstellen / rangieren
mean (v)	[miːn]	bedeuten / sagen wollen
meat products	[ˈmiːt ˌprɒdʌkts]	Fleischprodukte
member	[ˈmembə]	Mitglied
message	[ˈmesɪdʒ]	Nachricht
military	[ˈmɪlɪtri]	militärisch
minutes	[ˈmɪnɪts]	Protokoll
miscellaneous	[ˌmɪsəˈleɪniəs]	sonstig
misuse (v)	[ˌmɪsˈjuːz]	falsch einsetzen
mobile phone (UK)	[ˌməʊbaɪl ˈfəʊn]	Handy
mode of transport	[məʊd ɒf ˈtrænspɔːt]	Transportmittel
module	[ˈmɒdjuːl]	Modul
motorway / highway	[ˈməʊtəweɪ / ˈhaɪweɪ]	Autobahn
movement	[ˈmuːvmənt]	Bewegung
multi-modal transport	[ˌmʌlti ˈməʊdəl ˌtrænspɔːt]	Kombiverkehr

n

narrow	[ˈnærəʊ]	eng
native speaker	[ˈneɪtɪv ˌspiːkə]	Muttersprachler(in)
necessary	[ˈnesəsəri]	notwendig
negotiable	[nɪˈgəʊʃɪəbl]	übertragbar / begebbar
No. (number)	[ˈnʌmbə]	Anzahl
non-negotiable	[ˌnɒnnɪˈgəʊʃɪəbl]	nicht begebbar / nicht übertragbar

notify address	[ˈnəʊtɪfaɪ əˈdres]	Meldeadresse
nuclear power	[ˈnjuːklɪə ˈpaʊə]	Kernkraft

o

occupation	[ˌɒkjəˈpeɪʃən]	Beschäftigung / Beruf
occur (v)	[əˈkɜː]	geschehen
ocean currents	[ˈəʊʃən ˌkʌrənts]	Meeresströmungen
ocean vessel	[ˈəʊʃən ˌvesəl]	Seeschiff
offer	[ˈɒfə]	Angebot
offer (v)	[ˈɒfə]	anbieten
office accommodation	[ˈɒfɪs əˌkɒməˈdeɪʃən]	Büroräume
office hours	[ˈɒfɪs ˌaʊəz]	Arbeitsstunden
offshore	[ˈɒfʃɔː]	offshore / im Meer
oil	[ɔɪl]	Öl
old-fashioned	[ˌəʊldˈfæʃənd]	altmodisch
on board	[ˌɒn ˈbɔːd]	an Bord
on demand	[ˌɒn dɪˈmɑːnd]	auf Abruf
on purpose	[ɒn ˈpɜːpəs]	absichtlich
on receipt of	[ˌɒn rɪˈsiːt ɒf]	beim Empfang
on request	[ˌɒn rɪˈkwest]	auf Wunsch
on the contrary	[ɒn ðə ˈkɒntrəri]	im Gegenteil
operating costs	[ˈɒpəreɪtɪŋ ˌkɒsts]	Betriebskosten
opportunity	[ˌɒpəˈtjuːnəti]	Gelegenheit
opposite	[ˈɒpəzɪt]	Gegenteil
order	[ˈɔːdə]	Bestellung
order (v)	[ˈɔːdə]	bestellen
order number	[ˈɔːdə ˌnʌmbə]	Bestellungsnummer
organise (v)	[ˈɔːgənaɪz]	organisieren
otherwise	[ˈʌðəwaɪz]	sonst
out of order	[ˌaʊt ɒf ˈɔːdə]	außer Betrieb
out of stock	[ˌaʊt əf ˈstɒk]	ausverkauft
outgoing goods	[aʊtˈgəʊɪŋ ˌgʊdz]	Warenausgang
outsource (v)	[ˈaʊtsɔːs]	outsourcen/ auslagern
outsourcing	[ˈaʊtsɔːsɪŋ]	Outsourcing
overalls	[ˈəʊvərɔːlz]	Arbeitskleidung
oxidiser	[ˈɒksɪdaɪzə]	oxidierende Substanz

p

package	[ˈpækɪdʒ]	Paket
packaging	[ˈpækɪdʒɪŋ]	Verpackung
packer	[ˈpækə]	Verpacker(in)
packing case	[ˈpækɪŋ ˌkeɪs]	Kiste
pallet	[ˈpælɪt]	Palette
palletiser	[ˈpælətaɪzə]	Palettierer
part	[pɑːt]	Teil
participant	[pɑːˈtɪsɪpənt]	Teilnehmer(in)
participate (v)	[pɑːˈtɪsɪpeɪt]	teilnehmen
particle emission	[ˈpɑːtɪkl ɪˈmɪʃən]	Partikelemission / Teilchenemission

pass on (a message) (v)	[ˌpɑːs ˈɒn (ə ˈmesɪdʒ)]	weiterleiten
passenger	[ˈpæsəndʒə]	Passagier
payment	[ˈpeɪmənt]	Bezahlung
per day	[ˌpɜː ˈdeɪ]	pro Tag
period of notice	[ˈpɪərɪəd ɒf ˈnəʊtɪs]	Kündigungsfrist
perishable	[ˈperɪʃəbl]	verderblich
personnel	[pɜːsəˈnel]	Personal
persuade (v)	[pəˈsweɪd]	überzeugen
pharmaceutical industry	[ˌfɑːməˈsjuːtɪkəl ˈɪndəstri]	Pharmaindustrie
pharmaceutical products	[ˌfɑːməˈsjuːtɪkəl ˌprɒdʌkts]	Arzneimittel
pick (v) (goods in warehouse)	[pɪk (gʊdz ɪn ˈweəhaʊs)]	kommissionieren
pick up (v)	[ˌpɪk ˈʌp]	abholen
pick-up services	[ˈpɪkʌp ˌsɜːvɪsɪz]	Abholdienste
place of delivery	[ˌpleɪs ɒf dɪˈlɪvəri]	Entladeort
place of issue	[ˌpleɪs ɒf ˈɪʃuː]	Ausstellungsort
place of receipt	[ˌpleɪs ɒf rɪˈsiːt]	Übernahmeort
plant	[plɑːnt]	Werk
Please note!	[ˌpliːz ˈnəʊt]	Bitte merken!
plug in (v)	[ˌplʌg ˈɪn]	einstecken
point	[pɔɪnt]	Punkt
policy	[ˈpɒləsi]	Police
polite / politely	[pəˈlaɪt], [pəˈlaɪtli]	höflich
polluted	[pəˈluːtɪd]	verschmutzt
port	[pɔːt]	Hafen
port of discharge	[ˌpɔːt ɒf ˈdɪstʃɑːdʒ]	Löschhafen
port of loading	[ˌpɔːt ɒf ˈləʊdɪŋ]	Verschiffungshafen
post	[pəʊst]	Stelle
pour (v)	[pɔː]	gießen
practise (v)	[ˈpræktɪs]	üben
premium	[ˈpriːmiəm]	Prämie
prepare (v)	[prɪˈpɜə]	vorbereiten
prescription	[prɪˈskrɪpʃən]	Rezept (vom Arzt)
preserve (v)	[prɪˈzɜːv]	erhalten
press (v)	[pres]	drucken
prevent (v)	[prɪˈvent]	vermeiden
price	[praɪs]	Preis
print (v)	[prɪnt]	drucken
probably	[ˈprɒbəbli]	wahrscheinlich
proceedings	[prəˈsiːdɪŋz]	Verfahren
process	[ˈprəʊses]	Prozedur
process an order (v)	[ˈprəʊses ən ˈɔːdə]	einen Auftrag ausführen
processing facility	[ˈprəʊsesɪŋ fəˈsɪləti]	Aufbereitungsanlage
procurement	[prəˈkjʊəmənt]	Beschaffung / Anschaffung
produce (v)	[prəˈdjuːs]	herstellen / produzieren
profit margin	[ˈprɒfɪt ˌmɑːdʒɪn]	Gewinnspanne
project leader	[ˈprɒdʒekt ˌliːdə]	Projektleiter(in)
promise	[ˈprɒmɪs]	Versprechen
promise (v)	[ˈprɒmɪs]	versprechen
promote (v)	[prəˈməʊt]	befördern / fördern

proof	[pruːf]	Beweis
protect (v)	[prəʊˈtekt]	schützen
provide (v)	[prəˈvaɪd]	anbieten / zur Verfügung stellen
pull (v)	[pʊl]	ziehen
purchasing (department)	[ˈpɜːtʃəsɪŋ (dɪˈpɑːtmənt)]	Einkauf(sabteilung)
purpose	[ˈpɜːpəs]	Zweck
purpose-built	[ˌpɜːpəs ˈbɪlt]	für einen speziellen Zweck gebaut

q

quantity	[ˈkwɒntəti]	Menge
quarter	[ˈkwɔːtə]	Quartal
quay	[kiː]	Kai
questionnaire	[ˌkwestʃəˈneə]	Fragebogen
quota	[ˈkwəʊtə]	Kontingent
quote / quotation	[kwəʊt], [kwəʊˈteɪʃən]	Preisvorschlag / Angebot

r

rack	[ræk]	Regal
raft	[rɑːft]	Floß
rag	[ræg]	Lappen / Fetzen
rail	[reɪl]	Bahn
rail track	[ˈreɪl ˌtræk]	Eisenbahngleis
ramp	[ræmp]	Rampe
range	[reɪndʒ]	Palette / Assortiment
rate	[reɪt]	Preis / Tarif
raw material	[ˌrɔː məˈtɪəriəl]	Rohstoff
re.	[riː]	bezüglich / betreffs
react (v)	[riˈækt]	reagieren
ready-to-wear	[ˈredi tu ˈweə]	fertig zum Anziehen
receipt	[rɪˈsiːt]	Quittung
receive (v)	[rɪˈsiːv]	empfangen
recipient	[rɪˈsɪpiənt]	Empfänger
reckon (v)	[ˈrekən]	kalkulieren
recognise (v)	[ˈrekəgnaɪz]	erkennen
recognised	[ˈrekəgnaɪzd]	anerkannt
recommend (v)	[ˌrekəˈmend]	empfehlen
recommendation	[ˌrekəmenˈdeɪʃən]	Empfehlung
record (v)	[rɪˈkɔːd]	aufschreiben / aufnehmen
recruit (v)	[rɪˈkruːt]	Lehre / Lehrzeit
reefer	[ˈriːfə]	Kühlcontainer
refuse (v)	[rɪˈfjuːz]	verweigern
register (v)	[ˈredʒɪstə]	anmelden
registered	[ˈredʒɪstəd]	eingetragen
regulate (v)	[ˈregjəleɪt]	regulieren
regulation	[ˌregjəˈleɪʃən]	Vorschrift
reject (v)	[rɪˈdʒekt]	ablehnen, zurückweisen
relationship	[rɪˈleɪʃənʃɪp]	Beziehung
release	[rɪˈliːs]	Freigabe

reliable	[rɪˈlaɪəbl]	zuverlässig
remove (v)	[rɪˈmuːv]	entfernen / beheben
renewable	[rɪˈnjuːəbl]	erneuerbar
repeat (v)	[rɪˈpiːt]	wiederholen
replace (v)	[rɪˈpleɪs]	ersetzen
replenish (v)	[rɪˈplenɪʃ]	wieder auffüllen
reply (v)	[rɪˈplaɪ]	antworten
report	[rɪˈpɔːt]	Bericht
represent (v)	[ˌreprɪˈzent]	vertreten
reputation	[ˌrepjəˈteɪʃən]	Ruf
request (v)	[rɪˈkwest]	bitten / erbitten
require (v)	[rɪˈkwaɪə]	benötigen
requirements	[rɪˈkwaɪəmənts]	Anforderungen
researcher	[rɪˈsɜːtʃə]	Forscher
resident	[ˈrezɪdənt]	Einwohner
response	[rɪˈspɒns]	Antwort / Reaktion
responsibility	[rɪˌspɒnsəˈbɪləti]	Verantwortung
responsible for	[rɪˈspɒnsəbl ˌfɔː]	verantwortlich für
restrict (v)	[rɪˈstrɪkt]	begrenzen
retail shops	[ˈriːteɪl ˌʃɒps]	Einzelhandel
retail trade	[ˈriːteɪl ˌtreɪd]	Einzelhandel
revenue	[ˈrevənjuː]	Einkommen
ride (v) (a motorbike)	[raɪd (ə ˈməʊtəbaɪk)]	Motorrad fahren
ripen (v)	[ˈraɪpən]	reifen
risk	[rɪsk]	Risiko
road haulier	[ˌrəʊd ˈhɔːliə]	Frachtführer
road waybill	[ˈrəʊd ˌweɪbɪl]	Frachtbrief
roadworthiness	[ˈrəʊdˌwɜːðɪnəs]	Verkehrstauglichkeit
role	[rəʊl]	Rolle
route	[ruːt]	Route
rubber duck	[ˈrʌbə ˌdʌk]	Badespielzeug / Gummiente
rubbish	[ˈrʌbɪʃ]	Abfall
rule	[ruːl]	Regel
run	[rʌn]	Fahrt

S

sack	[sæk]	Sack
safe(ly)	[ˈseɪf(li)]	sicher
sailing ship	[ˈseɪlɪŋ ˌʃɪp]	Segelschiff
salary	[ˈsæləri]	Gehalt
sales	[seɪlz]	Verkäufe
salmon	[ˈsæmən]	Lachs
sample	[ˈsɑːmpl]	Muster
savings	[ˈseɪvɪŋz]	Ersparnisse
say goodbye (v)	[ˌseɪ gʊdˈbaɪ]	sich verabschieden
scarce	[skeəs]	knapp
schedule	[ˈʃedjuːl, ˈʃedʒuːl, ˈskedjuːl, ˈskedʒuːl]	Zeitplan
scheduled	[ˈʃedjuːld], [ˈʃedʒuːld], [ˈskedjuːld], [ˈskedʒuːld]	geplant

seal (v)	[siːl]	versiegeln
secure	[sɪˈkjʊə]	sicher
secure (v)	[sɪˈkjʊə]	sichern
security	[sɪˈkjʊərəti]	Sicherheit
selection	[sɪˈlekʃən]	Auswahl
sell (v)	[sel]	verkaufen
semi-trailer / articulated lorry	[ˈsemiˌtreɪlə / ɑːˌtɪkjəleɪtɪd ˈlɒri]	Sattelaufliege
sense	[sens]	Bedeutung
separate (v)	[ˈsepəreɪt]	teilen
several	[ˈsevərəl]	mehrere
shape	[ʃeɪp]	Form
shelf (plural: shelves)	[ʃelf], [ʃelvz]	Regal
shift (v)	[ʃɪft]	sich bewegen
ship (v)	[ʃɪp]	transportieren / verschiffen
shipment	[ˈʃɪpmənt]	Warensendung / Sendung
shipping note	[ˈʃɪpɪŋ ˌnəʊt]	Versandnote
short cut	[ˈʃɔːt ˌkʌt]	Abkürzung
short shipped	[ʃɔːt ʃɪpt]	fehlerhafte Teillieferung
short-term	[ˌʃɔːtˈtɜːm]	kurzfristig
show (v)	[ʃəʊ]	zeigen
shrink-wrap (v)	[ˈʃrɪŋkræp]	einschweißen
signature	[ˈsɪgnətʃə]	Unterschrift
sink (v)	[sɪŋk]	sinken
site	[saɪt]	Platz
size	[saɪz]	Größe
slash	[slæʃ]	Schrägstrich
slot	[slɒt]	Platz
smuggle (v)	[ˈsmʌgl]	schmuggeln
soap	[səʊp]	Seife
solution	[səˈluːʃən]	Lösung
solve (v)	[sɒlv]	lösen
space	[speɪs]	Raum
space shuttle	[ˈspeɪs ʃʌtl]	Raumfähre
specialise (v)	[ˈspeʃəlaɪz]	spezialisieren
specimen	[ˈspesəmən]	Muster
speed	[spiːd]	Geschwindigkeit
spend (v) time	[ˌspend ˈtaɪm]	Zeit verbringen
spoil (v)	[spɔɪl]	zerstören
spoke	[spəʊk]	Speiche
stack (v)	[stæk]	stapeln
staff	[stɑːf]	Personal
stage	[steɪdʒ]	Stadium
stamp	[stæmp]	Stempel
standard	[ˈstændəd]	Norm
standard conditions	[ˈstændəd kənˈdɪʃənz]	allgemeine Bedingungen
standstill	[ˈstændstɪl]	Stillstand
state (v)	[steɪt]	angeben
staying power	[ˈsteɪɪŋ ˌpaʊə]	Durchhaltevermögen
steady	[ˈstedi]	stetig / unverändert

Vocabulary (alphabetical order)

stern	[stɜːn]	Heck
stick to (v)	[ˈstɪk ˌtu]	sich halten an
sticker	[ˈstɪkə]	Aufkleber
stock	[stɒk]	Lagebestand
stock list / inventory	[ˈstɒk lɪst / ˈɪnvəntri / ɪnˈventəri]	Inventar
storage	[ˈstɔːrɪdʒ]	Lagerung
store	[stɔː]	Geschäft
store / shop	[stɔː], [ʃɒp]	Geschäft
stormy	[ˈstɔːmi]	stürmisch
stow (v)	[stəʊ]	stauen
strap (v)	[stræp]	festbinden
strawberry	[ˈstrɔːbəri]	Erdbeere
streamline (v)	[ˈstriːmlaɪn]	rationalisieren
stuff (v) (a container)	[stʌf (ə kənˈteɪnə)]	packen
sub-contractor	[ˌsʌbkənˈtræktə]	Subunternehmer
subject line	[ˈsʌbdʒɪkt ˌlaɪn]	Bezugszeile
successful	[səkˈsesfʊl]	erfolgreich
suggest (v)	[səˈdʒest]	vorschlagen
suggestion	[səˈdʒestʃən]	Vorschlag
suitable	[ˈsuːtəbl], [ˈsjuːtəbl]	passend
supervise (v)	[ˈsuːpəvaɪz]	beaufsichtigen
supplier	[səˈplaɪə]	Zulieferer
supplies	[səˈplaɪz]	Vorräte
supply (v)	[səˈplaɪ]	liefern / beliefern
supply chain	[səˈplaɪ ˌtʃeɪn]	Versorgungskette
surcharge	[ˈsɜːtʃɑːdʒ]	Zuzahlung
surface transport	[ˈsɜːfəs ˈtrænspɔːt]	Land- und Seetransport
survive (v)	[səˈvaɪv]	überleben

t

tachograph	[ˈtækəʊgrɑːf]	Tachograph / Fahrtenschreiber
tag	[tæg]	Tag / Etikett
tailor-made	[ˈteɪləmeɪd]	maßgeschnitten
take over (v)	[ˌteɪk ˈəʊvə]	übernehmen
taken in charge in good order and condition	[ˈteɪkən ɪn ˌtʃɑːdʒ ɪn ɡʊd ˈɔːdər ænd kənˈdɪʃən]	übernommen in einwandfreiem Zustand
tamper with (v)	[ˈtæmpə ˌwɪð]	fälschen
target /objective	[ˈtɑːgɪt], [əbˈdʒektɪv]	Ziel
tariff	[ˈtærɪf]	Tarif
task	[tɑːsk]	Aufgabe
telephone line	[ˈtelɪfəʊn laɪn]	Telefonleitung
telephone receiver	[ˈtelɪfəʊn rɪˈsiːvə]	Telefonhörer
temporary job	[ˌtempərəri ˈdʒɒb]	Aushilfsstelle
terrorism	[ˈterərɪzm]	Terrorismus
testimonial	[ˌtestɪˈməʊniəl]	Zeugnis
That sounds fantastic.	[ðæt saʊndz fænˈtæstɪk]	Das hört sich fantastisch an.
theft	[θeft]	Diebstahl
thick	[θɪk]	dick

thickness	[ˈθɪknəs]	Dicke
tick (v)	[tɪk]	mit einem Häkchen versehen
tick off (v)	[ˌtɪk ˈɒf]	abhaken
toilet cleaner	[ˈtɔɪlət ˌkliːnə]	WC-Reiniger
toll	[təʊl]	Maut
toxic	[ˈtɒksɪk]	giftig / Gift-
tracing and tracking	[ˈtreɪsɪŋ ænd ˈtrækɪŋ]	Sendungsverfolgung
trade	[treɪd]	Handel
trader	[ˈtreɪdə]	Händler
trailer	[ˈtreɪlə]	Anhänger
tramp ship	[ˈtræmp ʃɪp]	Trampschiff
transaction	[trænˈzækʃən]	Transaktion
transfer (a call)	[trænsˈfɜːr (ə kɔːl)]	durchstellen
transhipment	[trænzˈʃɪpmənt]	Umladung
treatment	[ˈtriːtmənt]	Behandlung
trial run	[ˈtraɪəl ˌrʌn]	Probelauf
trip	[trɪp]	Fahrt
troops	[truːps]	Truppen
tropical climate	[ˈtrɒpɪkəl ˌklaɪmət]	tropisches Klima
truck driver/ heavy goods vehicle driver/ lorry driver	[ˈtrʌk ˌdraɪvə / ˌhevi ˈɡʊdz ˌvɪəkl ˌdraɪvə / ˈlɒri ˌdraɪvə]	Lastwagenfahrer
trucker	[ˈtrʌkə]	Lastwagenfahrer
true	[truː]	wahr
trust (v)	[trʌst]	vertrauen
turning blades	[ˈtɜːnɪŋ ˌbleɪdz]	Rotorblätter

u

unfortunately	[ʌnˈfɔːtʃnətli]	leider
uniform	[ˈjuːnɪfɔːm]	einheitlich
unite (v)	[juːˈnaɪt]	vereinigen
unitised cargo	[ˈjuːnɪtaɪzd ˈkɑːɡəʊ]	Einheitsladung
unload (v)	[ʌnˈləʊd]	löschen / abladen
unsatisfactory	[ʌnˌsætɪsˈfæktəri]	nicht zufriedenstellend
urgent	[ˈɜːdʒənt]	dringend

v

vacation	[vəˈkeɪʃən]	Semesterferien
vague	[veɪɡ]	vage
valuable	[ˈvæljuəbl]	wertvoll
value	[ˈvæljuː]	Wert
variation	[ˌveəriˈeɪʃən]	Veränderung
VAT (value added tax)	[viː eɪ tiː (ˈvæljuː ˈædɪd tæks)]	MwSt (Mehrwertsteuer)
vegetables	[ˈvedʒətəblz]	Gemüse
vehicle	[ˈvɪəkl]	Fahrzeug
vehicle fleet	[ˈvɪəkl ˌfliːt]	Fuhrpark
ventilated	[ˈventɪleɪtɪd]	ventiliert
vet (veterinarian)	[vet (ˌvetərɪˈneəriən)]	Tierarzt
view	[vjuː]	Meinung
vocational training	[vəˈkeɪʃənəl ˈtreɪnɪŋ]	Berufsausbildung

W

wanted	[ˈwɒntɪd]	gesucht
warehouse	[ˈweəhaʊs]	Lager
warehouse (v)	[ˈweəhaʊz]	lagern
warehouse operative	[ˈweəhaʊs ˈɒpərətɪv]	Lagerarbeiter(in)
warehousing	[ˈweəhaʊzɪŋ]	Lagerung
waste	[weɪst]	Abfall
waste (v)	[weɪst]	verschwenden
waybill	[ˈweɪbɪl]	Frachtbrief
weapon	[ˈwepən]	Waffe
weed killer	[ˈwiːd ˌkɪlə]	Unkrautvertilgungsmittel
weigh (v)	[weɪ]	wiegen
weight	[weɪt]	Gewicht
wheel	[wiːl]	Rad
wide	[waɪd]	breit
width	[wɪdθ]	Breite
willing	[ˈwɪlɪŋ]	bereit
wind farm	[ˈwɪnd ˌfɑːm]	Windpark
without a hitch	[wɪˌðaʊt ə ˈhɪtʃ]	reibungslos
wonder (v)	[ˈwʌndə]	sich fragen
work placement	[ˈwɜːk ˌpleɪsmənt]	Praktikum
world	[wɜːld]	Welt
worry (v)	[ˈwʌri]	sich Sorgen machen
Would you mind …?	[ˌwʊd ju ˈmaɪnd]	Hätten Sie was dagegen …?

Bildquellenverzeichnis

Fotos

dpa Picture- alliance GmbH, Frankfurt: S. 57

Fotolia Deutschland GmbH, Berlin: S. 7 (Franck Boston), 8 (Monkey Business), 10.1 (Kadmy), 10.2 (gilles lougassi), 10.3 (robynmac), 10.4 (thomaslerchphoto), 10.5 (Kadmy), 10.6 (Pierre-Yves Babelon), 11 (il-fede), 13.1 (Unclesam), 13.2 (Thorsten Schier), 17.1 (Minerva Studio), 17.2 (adisa), 19 (ufotopixl10), 22 (Picture-Factory), 25 (Media Rocks), 29 (Dmytro Tolokonov), 34 (goodluz), 35.1 (Bergfee), 35.2 (il-fede), 38 (Elenathewise), 42 (lassedesignen), 45 (B. Wylezich), 48 (Jakob Kamender), 50.1 (nmann77), 50.2 (Masyanya), 52 (white), 53 (Karsten Thiele), 60.1 (soleg), 60.2 (jo), 65 (yukata), 69 (Herbert Rubens), 70 (Pierre-Yves Babelon), 72 (Alexander Raths), 76.2 (robepco), 79 (Addi30), 81 (kovaleff), 82 (osiris59), 94 (endostock), 95 (pressmaster), 99 (adistock), 100 (roostler), 101 (endostock), 104.1 (Kzenon), 104.2 (Monkey Business), 104.3 (maxoidos), 104.4 (minicel73), 108 (mimon), 111 (CHEN, PAO-CHIN), 113 (halberg), 115 (Scanrail), 118 (banhegyesi), 121 (apops), 124 (Jeanette Dietl), Umschlagfoto (Alfonso de Tomas)

Zeichnungen

Sally Ann Vollmers/Bildungsverlag EINS: S. 55